MODULE TWO

THE FINANCIAL ISSUES OF DIVORCE

Module Two: The Financial Issues of Divorce
Copyright © 2015 by CertiTrek Publishing
Printed in the United States of America
Published by CertiTrek Publishing

First printing March 1988	Eleventh printing May 2007
Second printing January 1994	Twelfth printing April 2010
Third printing May 1994	Thirteenth printing January 2011
Fourth printing February 1995	Fourteenth printing August 2011
Fifth printing December 1995	Fifteenth printing March 2012
Sixth printing October 1998	Sixteenth printing October 2012
Seventh printing April 2000	Seventeenth printing November 2013
Eighth printing January 2001	Eighteenth printing July 2014
Ninth printing January 2004	Nineteenth printing February 2015
Tenth printing July 2005	

WARNING/DISCLAIMER

This publication is designed to provide a general overview on various divorce issues. The application and effect of this information can change based on the facts and circumstances in each case. The information herein is provided with the understanding that the publisher and authors are not providing legal, accounting, tax, or other professional advice. This publication should not be utilized as a substitute for legal, accounting, or professional advice. If legal advice or other expert assistance is required, the services of a qualified professional must be sought. Even though Certified Divorce Financial Analyst® (CDFA™) professionals are aware of the law, they do not practice law and do not give legal advice.

IDFA makes no warranties, expressed or implied, regarding any publications, programs, or software. This material is to be utilized in conjunction with legal advice and other expert assistance. Because the program, software, and any publications are general in nature, each must be tailored to a specific situation. IDFA makes no representations regarding the effectiveness of these materials in specific legal, accounting, or other professional situations.

Address inquiries to:

Institute for Divorce Financial Analysts
2224 Sedwick Road, Suite 102
Durham, NC USA 27713
(800) 875-1760 • info@InstituteDFA.com • www.InstituteDFA.com

Self-Study Course Instructions

About the Course

The Certified Divorce Financial Analyst® course is designed to prepare you to become an expert on the financial aspects of divorce. You will receive four books (modules) for each of the four topics: *Module One: The Fundamentals of Divorce; Module Two: The Financial Issues of Divorce; Module Three: The Tax Issues of Divorce*; and *Module Four: Working as a CDFA: Case Studies.*

Preparing for the Examinations

Read each module thoroughly, and then complete the "Sample Test Questions and Answers" section in Modules One, Two, Three, and Four in order to prepare for your exams. The study time for each Module is typically about 20 to 25 hours for most candidates. Each module has a multiple choice exam (Modules 1–3 have 100 questions each and Module 4 has 50 questions). You will have two hours to complete each exam.

To become a Certified Divorce Financial Analyst, you must receive a minimum score of 70% on each of the four exams; you may retake an exam if you do not pass.

If you have any questions regarding these materials, please contact IDFA at (800) 875-1760.

Scheduling Your Exam at an Approved Testing Center

Please refer to the email and information you received after purchasing the course for details about finding an approved testing center and scheduling your exam. If you have any issues scheduling your exam, please call IDFA customer service at (800) 875-1760.

Examination and Retake Fees

The exam fee is included in your tuition. There is no additional charge to take the exam. If you fail the exam, you may retake it for a fee of $150 each time you retake the exam. There is no limit on the number of times you may retake the exam.

Day of the Exam

Please arrive at the testing center 15 minutes prior to your scheduled appointment time. You will be required to present two forms of identification, at least one of which must be a photo ID. Acceptable forms of photo ID include: state-issued driver's license, passport, military identification, an employee identification card, or a student picture ID from an accredited college or university. The following forms of non-photo ID are acceptable: credit card, check-cashing card, or a bank debit card. A social security card is not an acceptable form of identification.

What to Bring to an Exam

- Two forms of acceptable identification (see above for details).

- The authorization code you received in the confirmation email.

- One of the following permitted calculators: HP 10b, 10bII, 10bII+, 17bII+, 12c or TI BAII, BAII Plus, BAII Plus Professional.

What Will be Provided at the Exam

- Tax and life expectancy tables will be provided during the exam on your display in a split-screen format.

- Whiteboard.

TABLE OF CONTENTS

Chapter 1: Property 1

What constitutes property? 2

What is separate property vs. marital property?............................2

How do you inventory the assets? 3

How do you find hidden assets? 3

What is the value of the property?..7

Do career assets have value? 8

How will the assets be divided? 10

Community Property States 10

Equitable Distribution States... 10

Dividing Marital Property and Debt 13

The Family Business 14

Valuing the Business.. 14

Dividing the Business... 15

Equal vs. Equitable Property Division 16

Chapter 2: Retirement Plans 17

Defined Contribution Plans... 17

Vesting Calculations for Defined Contribution Plans.................. 18

Transferring Assets from a Defined Contribution Plan 19

Individual Retirement Accounts 21

Defined Benefit Plan 21

Methods of Dividing 21

Transferring Assets from a Defined Benefit Plan....................... 22

Case Studies: Three Different Parameters of the Defined Benefit.................... 24

Qualified Domestic Relations Order (QDRO) 26

Legislative Background... 27

QDRO Limitations 28

Public Employee Pensions 29

Discount Rate of Interest 30

Survivor Benefits 31

Vesting 31

Mature Plans 32

Double Dipping 32

The Carrot Story 33

The Pitfalls of Dividing Pensions 36

Chapter 3: The Marital Home 40

Options 42

Tax Issues – Sale of the Principal Residence........................... 45

Financial Viability of Keeping the Residence 48

Bob's Proposal – Scenario 1 55

Chapter 4: Spousal Support 68

Criteria for Receiving or Paying Spousal Support 69

Rehabilitative Maintenance.. 71

Modification of Spousal Support.. 72

Tax Issues of Spousal Support 73

Taxable vs. Non-taxable Spousal Support 76

Guaranteeing Spousal Support 78

Chapter 5: Child Support 80

Modifying Child Support 82

Income Tax Considerations 82

Child Contingency Rule 83

Discussion... 84

Recession-related Issues 85

Chapter 6: Social Security 86

Other Social Security Issues 88

Chapter 7: Insurance 90

Health Insurance And COBRA.. 90

Life Insurance 91

Chapter 8: Debt, Credit, and Bankruptcy.......................... 93

Debt... 93

Secured Debt.. 94

Unsecured Debt 94

Tax Debt 94

Qualified Principal Residence Indebtedness 95

Divorce Expenses 95

Credit... 95

Bankruptcy.. 96

Sample Test 98

Sample Tax Rates 152

Sample Life Expectancy.. 153

Glossary 154

CONTENT OUTLINE: MODULE 2

Chapter 1: Property

- Differentiate between marital and separate property in a divorce settlement.
- Recognize hidden assets by reviewing tax returns.
- Recognize hidden assets by reviewing other documents and transactions.
- Determine the value of property.
- Define a career asset.
- Recognize how assets and debt will be divided in a community property state versus an equitable distribution state.
- Outline the options for dividing a family business.
- Differentiate between an equitable distribution and an equal distribution.

Chapter 2: Retirement Plans

- Define what a defined contribution plan is and how they work.
- Determine the vested portion of a defined contribution plan.
- Explain how to transfer assets from a defined contribution plan.
- Recognize rules regarding dividing an IRA in a divorce.
- Recognize what a defined benefit plan is and how they work.
- Differentiate between the methods for dividing and transferring a pension.
- Calculate the present value of a pension, including the marital portion.
- Define what a QDRO is and how they work.
- State the importance of protecting survivor benefits.
- Associate the different vesting options with how they work.
- Recognize the common pitfalls of dividing a pension.

Chapter 3: The Marital Home

- Recognize the options for the marital home.
- Determine the cost basis of the marital home.
- Determine the capital gain on the sale of the home.

- Explain the rules regarding use and ownership periods.

- Determine the financial viability of keeping the residence.

- Review case studies to determine if one spouse can keep the residence.

Chapter 4: Spousal Support

- Outline the courts' criteria for ordering spousal support.

- Recognize what rehabilitative maintenance is and how it works.

- Determine whether spousal support is modifiable.

- Define the tax issues for spousal support.

- Define Taxable vs. Non-taxable support.

- Recognize what front-loading of spousal support is and how to avoid it.

- Explain the methods for guaranteeing spousal support.

Chapter 5: Child Support

- Explain with child support guidelines and their purpose.

- Specify how the non-custodial parent can claim the tax exemption.

- Define what the child contingency rules are and know how they work.

  - Six-month rule

  - Multiple reduction rule

Chapter 6: Social Security

- Explain how to qualify for spouse's Social Security benefits.

- Define what a spouse's rights are to Social Security benefits.

- Identify what happens when there are multiple spouses that qualify for benefits.

- Explain Social Security planning tips and issues.

Chapter 7: Insurance

- Discern what happens to health insurance and COBRA protections for divorcing couples.

- Explain how life insurance can be used.

Chapter 8: Debt, Credit, and Bankruptcy

- Associate rules regarding different kinds of debt.

- Secured debt
- Unsecured debt
- Tax debt
- Identify tax treatment and rules of Qualified Principal Residence Indebtedness.
- Interpret the rules regarding tax deductibility of divorce expenses.
- Define how credit and debt work in a divorce.
- Recognize the general rules regarding the types of bankruptcy.

CHAPTER 1
PROPERTY

Learning Objectives

After completing this chapter, you will be able to:

1. Describe the differences between separate and marital property.
2. Demonstrate how to inventory assets and recognize how to uncover hidden assets.
3. Calculate the value of property and allocate the value between the spouses.
4. Associate the differences in community property states and equitable distribution states with how they define and divide marital assets.
5. State the options for valuing and dividing a family business.
6. List the differences between equal and equitable property division.

When looking at the property issues in a divorce, a number of issues need to be considered. Below are some of the common questions individuals going through a divorce will ask:

- What constitutes property?

- What is separate property vs. marital property?

- How do you inventory the assets?

- How do you find hidden assets?

- What is the value of the property?

- Do career assets have value?

- How will the assets be divided?

- What is equal vs. equitable property division?

Although each couple is different, "most divorcing couples have household furnishings (89%), cars (71%), and some savings in the form of money in bank accounts, stocks, or bonds (61%). Almost half (46%) of the couples own or are buying a family home, which is likely to be a couple's most valuable asset. Only a small proportion of divorcing couples have a pension (24%), a business (11%), or other real estate (11%)."[1]

---

[1] The Divorce Revolution. *Lenore Weitzman, Chapter 3: "The Nature of Marital Property." The Free Press (A Division of Macmillan, Inc.), 1985.*

In recent years, research shows that couples are investing in their careers and earning capabilities instead of their savings accounts. They may see their careers as being more valuable than tangible assets. Because future income is typically of greater value than property, the main financial issues to consider, particularly for the non-working or lower-wage-earning spouse with children, are spousal and child support.

WHAT CONSTITUTES PROPERTY?

Property includes assets such as the family home, rental property, cars, boats, and art or antique collections. It also includes bank accounts, mutual funds, stocks and bonds, life insurance, cash value of life insurance, IRAs, retirement plans, stock options, non-qualified deferred compensation, and family-owned businesses. As you can see, there is virtually no limit as to what is considered property.

WHAT IS SEPARATE PROPERTY VS. MARITAL PROPERTY?

In some states, regardless of how property was brought into the marriage or whose name is on the title, all property of both spouses is subject to division and disposition at divorce. These states do not differentiate between marital and non-marital (or separate) property. However, the "source" of the property (gift, inheritance, or owned prior to marriage), while ignored when classifying the property, may be very important in the way in which the property is divided.

All states generally divide property to achieve fairness. The difference is the starting point and the rules each state uses to reach a fair result. For example, some states start from the standpoint that all property is subject to division by the court, and then, depending on the circumstances, give property that was owned prior to the marriage or was acquired by gift or inheritance to the party that owned or received it. Other states start with the notion that such property is not subject to distribution by the court at all, and thus narrow down the issues to be decided.

Although the laws vary from state to state, property is in most states usually divided into just two categories: separate and marital (sometimes called "community") property.

In general, separate property includes what a person:

- Brings into the marriage
- Inherits during the marriage
- Receives as a gift during the marriage

On the other hand, marital property is everything acquired during the marriage regardless of which spouse owns the property. In some states, marital property also includes the increase in value of separate property. Depending on the state, co-mingled separate property may be treated as separate or marital property.

HOW DO YOU INVENTORY THE ASSETS?

As explained in Module 1, one of the key roles of a CDFA professional is to work with clients to identify and collect financial data. You will be working with your client and his or her attorney to identify, collect, and evaluate the assets of the divorcing couple.

Clients will be in various stages of collecting the financial data. Some clients have been working with an attorney who has obtained and compiled the financial data and filed the data with the court. Other clients will meet with you prior to obtaining an attorney. As the CDFA professional, you are viewed as the financial expert and should be prepared to begin at any stage of the process.

In Module 1, there are several documents to assist you in the data collection process. Both spouses should complete these documents. The key documents for collecting information regarding the assets and liabilities are the financial affidavit and the asset/liability comparison worksheet.

HOW DO YOU FIND HIDDEN ASSETS?

The divorce process is a time of mistrust for each spouse. Right or wrong, each may accuse the other of hiding assets.

Assets are traditionally hidden in one of four ways:

- The person denies the existence of an asset.
- Assets are transferred to a third party.
- The person claims the asset was lost or dissipated.
- The person creates false debt.

It is the attorney's responsibility to organize and coordinate discovery. However, he or she may ask for your assistance. Here are some logical areas where financial expertise can help the attorney in generating the facts.

Tax returns are the first place to look to discover hidden assets. It is a good idea to look at tax returns for the past five years. By reviewing the tax returns you may discover assets that your client had no knowledge of or that were not disclosed by your client's spouse. The first two pages of a tax return can serve as a "table of contents," because they list the forms and schedules that are attached to the return.

Important forms to review include:

- **Schedule A – Itemized Deductions**. This form may help identify unlisted assets or sources of income. For example, property taxes may reveal real property or a boat that one spouse does not know exists; and gambling losses would reveal that there are gambling winnings.

- **Schedule B – Interest and Ordinary Dividends**. This identifies the assets and investments generating interest and dividends.

- **Schedule C – Profit or Loss From Business**. This form may be a place to hide assets or income. For example, depreciation expense is not a cash outflow and should sometimes be added back to net income to determine the actual income. The depreciation schedule may also reveal additional assets in the business.

- **Schedule D – Capital Gains and Losses**. This form is used to report gains and losses from the sale of stocks, bonds, and real estate.

- **Schedule E – Supplemental Income and Loss**. This form is used to report income from rental properties, royalties, and partnership and S-corporation income. Depreciation would be something to review.

- **Form 1065** is used to report partnership income.

- **Forms 1120 and 1120S** are used to report corporate income.

You need to review the federal and state income tax returns, as well as all 1099s and W-2s. Amended returns should also be reviewed.

Assets have a way of disappearing after divorce proceedings start. One of the first tasks your client needs to complete is to list what assets he or she thinks the two of them own. That list should include:

- **Cash**. Does your client or his or her spouse keep substantial amounts of cash at home or in a safety deposit box?

- **Checking accounts**. The list should include personal, joint, business, or trust accounts. If you have reason to believe your client's spouse is hiding assets, you should go over all the canceled checks and bank statements for the past few years and post the expenditures under the appropriate column (e.g., mortgage, utilities, car payments, other loans, entertainment).

- **Savings or money-market accounts**. Don't forget accounts set up for a "special purpose" such as Christmas, clubs, or annual or semiannual expenses. Those accounts are usually funded by payroll deduction and are set up to fund large and infrequent expenses such as property taxes, the annual premium on the home, auto insurance, Christmas, and so on. These accounts are easy to forget. If possible, review the passbooks or monthly statements for all accounts open during the past five years.

- **Children's bank accounts**: Find out whether the spouse has recently opened custodial accounts in the name of one or more children.

- **Retirement accounts**. These include IRAs, defined contribution plans, and pension plans (government and private). Don't forget any plans from previous employers that were left behind.

- **Non-retirement investment accounts**. These include mutual funds, brokerage accounts, annuities, cash-value of life insurance, certificates of deposit, and stocks or bonds held in certificate form.

- **Real estate**. The main asset is usually the family home. Any other property owned by the couple—vacation homes, rentals, vacant land, and business property—should be included.

- **Employer-funded incentive programs**. These include stock-option programs, country club initiation fees, accumulated vacation, and sick days.

- **Deferred pay-raises or bonuses**. Check with the employer to discover when the spouse is due for a raise, how much that increase is likely to be, and whether he or she has earned bonuses or commissions that has not been collected.

Once you have helped your client to complete this list, ask him or her to start collecting statements for every item on it. Investment companies send monthly or quarterly statements, depending on the type of account, the level of trading activity, and the company's policy. Most employer-sponsored plans send out a year-end statement in the first quarter of the following year, so don't panic if a statement you are looking for does not show up at the end of the first month after you start the process. If your client has a safety deposit box, ask him or her to visit the bank and make a list of its contents. Ideally, your client would know what should be in the box and be able to list items that have mysteriously disappeared. Lastly, ask your client to make a copy of the last mortgage closing paperwork. In order to qualify for a mortgage, your client and his or her spouse should have disclosed all of their assets, liabilities, and sources of income, as well as the last five years' tax returns. Tax returns will show the sources and amount of income, especially if one spouse is self-employed.

The following information has been excerpted from *The Divorce Handbook* written by James T. Friedman, which is a valuable resource for financial planners assisting their clients during a divorce. Mr. Friedman is a specialist in family law. Since 1970 he has been regularly engaged in drafting family-law-related legislation on behalf of the Illinois State Bar

Association, the Chicago Bar Association, and the American Academy of Matrimonial Lawyers.[2]

In the course of discovery (sharing documents and financial information with the opposing side), most spouses believe that their counterpart has somehow hidden or failed to disclose the existence of certain assets. The following checklist of research items may assist in determining the whereabouts of hidden assets or if, in fact, they exist at all:

1. **Financial Statements (loans from lending institutions)**

2. **Personal Income Tax Returns**

3. **Corporate Income Tax Returns**

4. **Partnership Income Tax Returns**

5. **Canceled Checks and Check Registers from Personal, Partnership, and Corporate Accounts**

6. **Savings Account Passbooks**

7. **Security or Commodity Account Statements**

8. **Expense Accounts**

9. **Deferred Salary Increase, Uncollected Bonus, or Commissions**

10. **Safe Deposit Box Activity**

11. **Cash Transactions and In Kind Compensation**

12. **Children's Bank Accounts**

13. **Personal Knowledge of Spouse's Habits**

14. **Phony Income Tax Return**

15. **Phony Loans or Debts**

16. **"Friends" or Other Phonies on the Payroll**

17. **Retirement Plan Abuse**

18. **Defined Benefit Pension Plans**

19. **Estate, Gift, and Inheritance Tax Returns[3]**

---

[2] The Divorce Handbook. *James T. Friedman, Chapter 7, "Financial Hide-and-Seek with Your Spouse," pages 49–53. Random House, 1982, 1984.*

WHAT IS THE VALUE OF THE PROPERTY?

To explain how property is valued and how to allocate the value between the spouses, we will look at examples similar to those you are likely to encounter in your practice.

Let's look at an example. Beth and her husband are getting a divorce and live in a state with marital and separate property. Assume that when Beth got married, she had $1,000 in a savings account. During the marriage, her $1,000 earned $100 in interest and now the account is worth $1,100.

Her property is $1,000 because she kept it in her name only, and in some states, the $100 in interest goes into the pot of marital assets to be divided because that is the increase in value of her separate property. If Beth had put her husband's name on the account, she would have turned the entire account into a marital asset. She would have made what is called a "presumptive gift" to the marriage.

In second or third marriages, both people may bring a house into the marriage. Suppose that Beth had a house when she got married, which she kept in her name only. At that time, the house was worth $100,000 and had a mortgage of $70,000, so the equity was $30,000. Now Beth is getting divorced. Today the house is worth $150,000. The mortgage is down to about $50,000. Equity has increased to $100,000.

	At Marriage		At Divorce
Value	$100,000	Value	$150,000
Mortgage	− 70,000	Mortgage	− 50,000
Equity	$30,000	Equity	$100,000

The increase in value is the increase in the equity, or $70,000.

Let's reverse the situation. Assume Beth put her husband's name on the deed to the house when they got married. After all, they were going to be together for the rest of their lives. As soon as she put her husband's name on the deed, she gave a presumptive gift to the marriage. This turned the house into a marital asset.

Now assume that Beth's aunt died and left her an inheritance of $10,000. If she put it into an account under her name, then at the divorce, it is her separate property except for the increase in value. It is the same with a gift. When she received the gift or inheritance, if she put it into a joint account, she turned that money into marital property.

Beth saves $100 of her paycheck every month. She puts this money into an account under her name only, and now it is worth $2,600. At her divorce, is this money separate or marital property? It is marital property because it was acquired during the marriage, regardless of whose name is on the account.

When Beth got married, her husband gave her an eight-carat diamond ring. Assume that they are in court and she is testifying that the ring was a gift from her husband so it is her separate property. He says, "Are you kidding? I would not give you an eight-carat diamond. That was an investment, so it is marital property." It is up to the judge to decide if the ring is marital property or separate property.

What if Beth's husband had given her an $80,000 painting for her birthday? She claimed it was a gift, and he claimed it was an investment and, therefore, should be treated as marital property. The judge could consider it an investment. Because it is not the type of thing that most people would freely give as a gift, it could be viewed as an investment for the family. The judge could consider the painting marital property. But remember, you can never predict what the judge will decide.

What happens when both parties want the same item? Beth and her husband divided all of their property except for one item. They could not agree who was going to get the set of antique crystal that they purchased in England. They both wanted it so badly that they ended up spending $60,000 in court to decide that one issue. This may seem absurd, but it happens every day. One of the roles of a CDFA professional is to insert reason and logic. At $60,000, they could have each bought a new set of crystal and a trip to England!

Generally, home furnishings are not included on the list of assets because the couple will simply divide the items. If they are to be valued, the typical value is what you could get if the items were sold at a garage sale.

DO CAREER ASSETS HAVE VALUE?

With many couples, one spouse has significant assets tied to his or her career. These career assets include:

- Life insurance
- Health insurance
- Disability insurance
- Vacation pay
- Sick pay
- Social Security benefits
- Unemployment benefits
- Stock options

- Pension plans

- Retirement savings plans

- Promotions

- Job experience

- Seniority

- Professional contacts

- Education

In many cases, a complete financial analysis may require that career assets be considered in arriving at an equitable settlement. Your client's attorney will know whether the judges in your state will consider career assets as part of the property settlement. For example, take a family in which the husband is the sole wage earner. Many times, the wife put the husband through school or helped him become established. At the same time, she abandoned or postponed her own education in the process. She may have quit her job to move from job to job with him. Together, they have made the decision to spend the time and energy to build his career with the expectation that she will share in the fruits of her investment through her husband's enhanced earning power. Over time, he has built up career assets that are part of what he earns even though they may not be paid directly to him.

Even in two-income families, one spouse's career often takes priority. Both spouses expect to share the rewards of that decision, at least, in the beginning of their marriage.

Some states even place a value on degrees such as a medical, dental, or law degrees.

A case in 1998 involved Lorna and Gary Wendt. It was a highly-publicized battle over career assets and even made the cover of Fortune magazine. He was the CEO of GE Capital; she was a "corporate wife."

The Wendts, married after both graduated from the University of Wisconsin, began with a net worth of $2,500. She gave up her career as a music teacher after her husband graduated from Harvard Business School. Lorna's Ph.T., or "Putting Hubby Through" degree, was introduced as evidence at the divorce proceedings.

At the time of the divorce, he declared their marital estate to be worth $21 million and offered her $8 million as her share. She argued that the estate was worth $100 million and she wanted half – $50 million. Her position was that his future pension benefits and stock options had been earned during their marriage. She said that her contribution as the homemaker and wife of the CEO enabled him to rise through the ranks to the top of his organization.

The Wendt case broke through the long-held belief that "enough is enough," that a spouse deserved enough to maintain her lifestyle, but nothing more. In a landmark decision, the judge awarded her $20 million – far less than the $50 million she asked for, but far more than the $8 million her husband initially offered. She also received $250,000 per year in alimony.

HOW WILL THE ASSETS BE DIVIDED?

Statutory Issues

The division of assets in a divorce is dependent upon the statutes governing property division in the state in which the divorcing couple resides. States have adopted two different types of property division statutes: community property and equitable distribution. There are state-to-state variations in these statutes, so you must learn the details of how your state(s) handles property division. Once you do that, you can work with your client and their attorney to prepare an asset list separating marital property, each spouse's individual property, and, in some situations, "to be determined" property.

COMMUNITY PROPERTY STATES

In community property states, the two spouses' "separate property" is not subject to division of the court. Generally speaking, separate property is owned before the marriage or obtained by gift or inheritance; everything else is "community property" and will likely be subject to a 50/50 division. When in doubt, most states presume that the "community" owns the property. Any property acquired in a community property state retains its community property status no matter where the couple moves. There are currently eight states that have adopted community property laws: Arizona, California, Idaho, Louisiana, Nevada, New Mexico, Texas, and Washington. Alaska has an optional community property act (AS 34.77.090), and Wisconsin is essentially a community property state, but there are exceptions to the typical community property rules. A mnemonic for remembering which states have community property laws is TWIN CAN LAW; remind yourself that the last two (AW, Alaska and Wisconsin) have special and unique treatment.

EQUITABLE DISTRIBUTION STATES

Equitable distribution states, on the other hand, usually agree that the couple's property, "marital property," is divided between the husband and wife equitably, or fairly. This does not necessarily mean 50/50. There are two types of equitable distribution states. They are differentiated by the way they identify property.

Martha and Tom

Martha and Tom have been married for 35 years. She stayed home and took care of their four children. Tom earns $150,000 per year and has started a business in the basement of their house. He expects the new business will bring in revenue after he retires. They own their house, which is worth $135,000. It is paid off. His pension has been valued at $90,000. Their savings account has $28,000, and Tom values the basement business at $75,000. Their assets total $328,000. Assuming a 50/50 property split, each would receive $164,000.

These are their assets:

House	$135,000
Pension	90,000
Savings	28,000
Business	75,000
Total	**$328,000**

However, splitting the property and assets down the middle is often not the most equitable division. In this case, Martha wants the house. Put it in her column on the property settlement worksheet.

Tom asks for his pension, which is placed in his column. He also says, "I have a business deal coming up soon and I am going to need cash for that deal. I must have the savings account." Put the savings account in his column.

Then Tom says, "The business in the basement is mine. You don't know what it looks like and you don't even have an idea of what I do." Put the business in his column.

Here's what the property settlement worksheet looks like.

		Martha	Tom
House	$135,000	$135,000	
Pension	90,000		$90,000
Savings	28,000		28,000
Business	75,000		75,000
Total	**$328,000**	**$135,000**	**$193,000**

Her assets total $135,000, and his assets total $193,000. If we were to look at a 50/50 property split, he would owe her $29,000. Although Tom has a large income of $150,000 a year, he does not want to give up any of the business, pension, or savings.

We can even out this division with a property settlement note. Tom can pay Martha $29,000 over time, like a note at the bank. He can make monthly payments with current market interest. Or, he can borrow funds directly from the bank since he has assets, including a savings account comparable to what he would owe.

A property settlement note is from the payor to the payee for an agreed-upon length of time with reasonable interest. It is still considered division of property, so the payor does not deduct it from taxable income. The payee does not pay taxes on the principal – only on the interest. It is important to collateralize this note.

If there is no other asset available, it is possible to collateralize this note with a qualified pension by using a Qualified Domestic Relations Order (QDRO). If the payor defaults on the payments of a property settlement note, then the payee can start collecting from the pension pursuant to the terms of the QDRO.

Martha does not like this settlement. She says, "I want the house and I want half of your pension. We have been married for 35 years, and I helped you earn that pension." Place the house ($135,000) in her column and $45,000 of the pension in each column. Then she says, "I want half of the savings account. You are not going to leave me without any cash." Put $14,000 in her column and $14,000 in Tom's column. She agrees that the business is Tom's, so $75,000 is placed in his column. The property split now looks like this:

		Martha	Tom
House	$135,000	$135,000	
Pension	90,000	45,000	$45,000
Savings	28,000	14,000	14,000
Business	75,000		75,000
Total	**$328,000**	**$194,000**	**$134,000**

Her assets are valued at $194,000, his at $134,000. Martha owes Tom $30,000 to make a 50/50 property settlement. It is not that simple. She does not have a job, has arthritis, and cannot walk very well. In reality, Martha is not in good health and it is unlikely she would be able to get a job that pays above minimum wage.

Her largest asset is the house, an illiquid asset. It is paid for, but it does not create revenue to buy groceries. She could rent out rooms for additional income, but that rarely works, and it creates a different lifestyle that she may not want. How is she going to pay $30,000 to Tom? The prospects are bleak. Given that Martha is in her mid-50s, has never worked outside the home, and her largest asset is illiquid, the parties may decide that this unequal division may be considered the most equitable.

Calculating spousal support comes after the property is divided. The reason for this is that support can be based on the amount of property received, so it is important to look first at the property division.

DIVIDING MARITAL PROPERTY AND DEBT

Many people try to divide each asset as they discuss it ("Your half of the house is $4,000, my half of the house is $4,000."). Since clients rarely divide the house like this, this may not be the most useful way to go about it. It may be more practical to begin listing each asset as a whole under the name of the person who will keep it. For example, in the wife's column, list the marital equity in the house if she is thinking of continuing to live there. List the entire value of the husband's retirement in his column, if that is the initial inclination. An advantage to this method is that it allows the client to see the balance (or lack of balance) of the initial plan as it is developed.

If the client wants to know dollar values, they may need a third party, such as an appraiser, to determine the value.

This is the time for the client to have a real heart-to-heart discussion with the ex-spouse and/or his or her attorney about the range of their sense of fairness and how the law would see the property division issues. Ask:

- Is the only possibility a 50/50 division of assets by value?

- Is one spouse more interested in cash than in other assets?

- Will one spouse take less than 50% if his or her share is all in cash?

- Is one spouse more interested in future security than in present assets?

- Is one spouse willing to wait for a buy-out of his or her share of the house or retirement assets? Is he or she looking for more than 50% to compensate for waiting?

- Will they settle for a "lopsided" agreement (more to one than the other) to compensate for the larger earnings of one of them now?

- Do they want to be "made whole" – end up where they were at the beginning of the relationship?

- Does one want to be compensated "off the top" for some contribution he or she made to the acquisition of property?

- Is there a possibility that there are any hidden assets or investments?

- What is the law?

If you can get them to agree on a plan that meets both spouses' idea of fairness, then it is much easier to come to a settlement.

As you allocate the debts, decide first whether they are marital, separate, or a mix. Then agree who will pay off the balance of each. Remember that the problem of unsecured debts may be more easily handled as a budget item rather than a division of property.

Think beyond the short term to the long-term effect of the division of assets and debts you are considering. For example, suppose one spouse gets all assets that appreciate slowly or depreciate and which take money to maintain (home, car, furniture, etc.). Then suppose the other spouse takes all the assets that increase in value or produce income (stock, retirement accounts, rental home, etc.). In such a case, even a few years after the divorce, what in the short term appeared to be a fair or equal division will look quite different. The net worth of the second spouse will far exceed the net worth of the first, and the gap will just continue to widen. It becomes your responsibility as a financial professional to assemble the financial facts and assumptions for your client to evaluate settlement options fully.

THE FAMILY BUSINESS

Whenever one of the marital assets in a divorce is a business, there are challenges in dividing the business or business assets. A business can be anything from dentistry, medicine, or law, to real estate or a home-based business. It can be a sole proprietorship, a partnership, or a corporation.

VALUING THE BUSINESS

Becky and James were getting a divorce after 35 years of marriage. James owned a heavy construction business. He agreed to split the assets 50/50 and said that the CPA at work valued the business at $300,000. Becky told her attorney, "I used to keep the books in the business for James, and we took in more than a million dollars each year. Do you think it would only be worth $300,000?"

Fortunately, Becky's attorney insisted that she have the business appraised. The appraisal cost Becky $8,300, and it made her very nervous to spend so much money. But the appraisal valued the company at $850,000, so her investment of $8,300 netted her $275,000 more than she would have received with the $300,000 value.

In a divorce situation, it is imperative to have the business appraised. Becky was right to question the value of the business because the CPA at her husband's business determined the value. There are Certified Business Appraisers (CBAs) who value businesses. To earn this designation, appraisers must pass a rigorous written exam and submit appraisals for review by a committee of experienced peers.

DIVIDING THE BUSINESS

There are generally three options for dividing the business: one spouse keeps the business, both spouses keep the business, or they sell the business outright and divide the proceeds.

One Spouse Keeps the Business

This is the most common solution and works best for most couples. In Becky and James's case, it was pretty clear that James ran the business, so he would keep the business and buy out Becky's interest or give her other assets of equal value. If there are no assets large enough to give her, he could sign a property settlement note to pay her over time.

If Becky owned shares of the company, the company could buy back her shares over time. However, there could be some significant tax consequences if the stock purchase is not structured properly. If there has been an increase in the value of the stock, Becky could be liable for capital gains tax. If James bought her shares directly, it would be considered a transfer of property "incident to divorce," which is not a taxable event. James's cost basis in the stock would be Becky's basis in the stock. James would not recognize gain until he sells the stock.

In a professional business, such as dentistry, medicine, or law, only the spouse that is the licensed professional can own the business.

Both Spouses Continue to Work in the Business

On the other hand, it is much more difficult to divide a family-owned business where the husband and wife have worked next to each other every day for years. They both have emotional ties with the business. In addition, trying to divide the business may kill it. Some couples are better business partners than marriage partners and are able to continue to work together in a business after the divorce is final. However, this will not work for everyone.

Sell the Business

Another option is to sell the business and divide the proceeds. This way, both parties are free to look elsewhere for another business or even to retire. However, it may be difficult to find a buyer; sometimes it takes years to sell a business. In the meantime, until the business is sold, decisions must made as to whether or not both spouses want to continue working in the business.

Stella and Dan owned a national franchise fast-food business. They also owned the land and the building. They worked hard to make this business a success. When they divorced, it was a difficult decision, but they finally agreed that Dan would take the business and Stella would take the land and building. This decision made Stella the landlord, which allowed her to control the rent from the business and the repairs and maintenance on the building. They soon realized they had made a bad decision. It cost them additional money to have their attorneys hammer out a new agreement. The new agreement allowed Dan to keep the business and the property and gave Stella enough cash to move out of the area and start over in a new location.

EQUAL VS. EQUITABLE PROPERTY DIVISION

Property divisions can be likened to trading. You trade assets back and forth until the couple agrees on the division. Or, in an equitable property division state, it means splitting the property equitably. It does not necessarily mean "equal." It means "fair."

Equitable = Fair, Not Equal

The word "equality" suggests fairness and equity for all parties involved, and parties can see this issue differently. An equal division of property may force the sale of family assets, especially the family home, so that the proceeds can be divided between the two spouses. The net result can be increased dislocation and disruption, especially in the lives of minor children. This may not be fair, in that the needs and interests of the children are not considered.

A second problem of "equitable is equal" is that a 50/50 division of property may not produce equal results—or equal standards of living after the divorce—if the two spouses are unequally situated at the time of divorce. This is most evident in the situation of the older homemaker. After a marital life devoted to homemaking, she is typically without substantial skills and experience in the workplace. Most likely, she will require a greater share of the property to cushion the income loss she suffers at divorce. Rarely is she in an equal economic position at divorce.

Generally, a 50/50 division is a starting point when property is divided in an equitable distribution state. A major consideration can be how much separate property the client has. Assume your client is fortunate enough to have $2 million in separate property, and that the marital estate totals $200,000. The $2 million separate property may mean that a 50% division of the marital property is inequitable.

CHAPTER 2
RETIREMENT PLANS

Learning Objectives

After completing this chapter, you will be able to:

1. Explain how retirement plans are generally divided between spouses upon divorce.
2. Calculate the vested portion of a defined contribution plan.
3. Recognize the rules regarding Individual Retirement Accounts (IRAs) in divorce.
4. Value and divide defined benefit plans among the spouses.
5. Define what a Qualified Domestic Relations Order (QDRO) is and how it works.
6. Define survivor benefits, vesting, and "double dipping."
7. Recognize potential pitfalls of dividing retirement plans.

Retirement plans are assets that are generally divided between the spouses upon divorce—unless part of the plan is considered separate property. Pension and retirement benefits that are earned during the marriage are potentially of great value. In a long-term marriage, the retirement plans may be the couple's most valuable asset.

There is a bewildering array of basic plans, with countless diverse provisions. Anyone who has tried to explain retirement plans and pensions knows that these plans are often very confusing.

There are two main types of qualified plans: defined contribution plans and defined benefit plans (pensions). Here is a very basic explanation of the two types and how they work. This basic information is very important when presenting different options to clients.

DEFINED CONTRIBUTION PLANS

It is very easy to determine the value of a defined contribution plan. Monthly or quarterly statements show the dollar amount available to be divided. Defined contribution plans have cash value today. They issue statements that indicate an actual dollar value of the account.

They can be divided equally or unequally by using a Qualified Domestic Relations Order (QDRO). Some companies allow an account to be divided so that the ex-spouse also has an account with the company. Otherwise, the defined contribution plan can be transferred to an Individual Retirement Account (IRA) for the ex-spouse without triggering tax consequences.

One of the most common types of defined contribution retirement plans is the 401(k) plan. Keep in mind 401(k) plans are very different because each company can set its own rules. The IRS must approve each plan.

VESTING CALCULATIONS FOR DEFINED CONTRIBUTION PLANS

Here are three examples of different employer contributions and how to calculate the vested amount for these types of defined contribution plans.

Employee A, who has been married for five years, works for a company that has a defined contribution plan. He puts all of his retirement money into the plan, and the company does not match any of his funds. He has worked there for three years and he has accumulated $1,500 in his plan. Any money that an employee puts into his plan is the employee's money; he or she is 100% vested. If he quits or is fired, he can take all of this money with him. He can use it as income and declare it to the IRS (and most likely be subject to the 10% penalty on the withdrawn amount) or he can roll it over to an IRA. After working for the company for three years, he and his wife are in the process of getting a divorce.

	Employee A
Length of employment	3 years
Value at time of divorce	$1,500
Percent vested	100%
Marital portion	$1,500

Employee B, who has also been married for five years, works for a company where only the employer contributes money to the defined contribution plan. The employee does not contribute to the plan. He has worked there for three years, and his plan is worth $1,500. The company uses a vesting schedule, which regulates how much money he can take with him if he quits or is fired. The amount depends on how long he has worked for the company. Employee B is 40% vested. Therefore, his plan today is worth 40% of $1,500 or $600. The lower amount, $600, is assigned to the marital pot of assets.

	Employee A	Employee B
Length of employment	3 years	3 years
Value at time of divorce	$1,500	$1,500
Percent vested	100%	40%
Marital portion	$1,500	$600

Employee C, also married for five years, works for a company that matches every dollar he puts in his plan with 50 cents. He has worked there for three years and he has $1,500 in his plan. Out of $1,500, he has put in $1,000 and the company has put in $500 with its matching program. He is 40% vested. The amount he contributed ($1,000) is 100% vested, and he can take the entire $1,000. He can only take 40% of the matched portion ($500), or $200. So Employee C's marital portion in his plan is worth $1,200.

	Employee A	Employee B	Employee C
Employee/employer contribution	0	100%	$1/50 cents
Length of employment	3 years	3 years	3 years
Value at divorce	$1,500	$1,500	$1,500
Percent vested	100%	40%	40%
Marital portion	$1,500	$600	$1,200

These examples illustrate different types of vesting for defined contribution plans. The company decides what it will contribute to the plan and decides the vesting schedule as permitted by the Internal Revenue Code.

TRANSFERRING ASSETS FROM A DEFINED CONTRIBUTION PLAN

Generally, a distribution made before a participant is age 59 ½ is an early distribution and subject to a 10% penalty. Some exceptions to the early distribution rules include distributions upon death or disability, distributions for medical expenses or qualified higher education expenses, distributions in the form of annuity payments for the life expectancy of the individual, or distributions made to an ex-spouse by a QDRO.

Internal Revenue Code Section (72)(t)(2)(C) allows money to be taken out of a qualified plan in accordance with a written divorce instrument (a QDRO). The recipient can spend any or all of the qualified money without paying the 10% penalty. However, the distribution is subject to ordinary income tax. When the ex-spouse takes a distribution, the plan has to withhold 20% for income taxes.

Esther just divorced her husband, an airline pilot who is nearing retirement. They are both age 55. There is $640,000 in his 401(k) and, according to the decree, she is to get $320,000 from the retirement plan. The administrator is prepared to transfer $320,000 from the 401(k) to her IRA.

She has decided to transfer the money to an IRA to avoid paying tax and penalties on this amount until retirement, when she will withdraw funds from the IRA. But Esther's attorney's fees are $60,000, and she needs another $20,000 to fix her house. So she held back $80,000 of the monies before transferring the remaining amount into her IRA – and she was able to receive the $80,000 without incurring the 10% penalty.

The problem is that because the plan administrator will withhold 20% of the distribution for taxes on the withdrawal, Esther should have asked for $100,000. If she had asked for $100,000, after the 20% withholding, she would have had $80,000 in cash and $220,000 to transfer to her IRA. Instead, she will pay 20% in taxes on her withdrawal and only receive $64,000 in cash. This will not cover both her attorney's fees and house repairs.

Once the money from a retirement plan is transferred into an IRA, you cannot take additional distributions from the IRA without paying the 10% penalty. This is because the IRA is not considered a qualified plan. So, if Esther later decides that she needs another $10,000 to buy a car, she will have to pay the 10% penalty, as well as the taxes on that money.

It is important to understand the difference between rolling over money from a qualified plan and transferring money from a qualified plan. The Unemployment Compensation Amendment Act (UCA), which took effect in January 1993, states that any monies taken out of a qualified plan or tax-sheltered annuity would be subject to 20% withholding. This rule does not apply to IRAs or SEPs.

In other words, if money is transferred from a qualified plan to an IRA, the check is sent directly from the qualified plan to the IRA. In a rollover, the funds are paid to the person who then remits the money to an IRA. A payment to the person, whether or not there is a rollover, is subject to the 20% withholding. Only a direct transfer avoids the withholding tax.

Here's an example of this: Henry was to receive his ex-wife Ginny's 401(k) of $100,000, which was invested in the ABC Mutual Fund. He asked the ABC Fund to send him the money directly so he could do a rollover into a different mutual fund of his choice. The ABC Fund sent Henry $80,000, which was the amount remaining after they withheld the mandatory 20% withholding tax.

Henry deposited the $80,000 in his new IRA mutual fund. Since he did it this way, the $20,000 that was withheld is considered a withdrawal and subject to tax. To avoid paying tax on the $20,000 withholding, he could have added $20,000 of his own money. Unfortunately, he did not have $20,000 to spare even though the IRS would have refunded that amount to him after filing his taxes.

Since he could not come up with the additional $20,000, when he filed his next tax return, he paid an extra $6,600 in state and federal taxes due to the $20,000. Of course, when it was time to file his tax return, $20,000 in taxes was already paid.

If Henry had instead transferred the $100,000 from the ABC Mutual Fund directly to his new fund, he would have $100,000 in his new fund (instead of $80,000) and would have saved $6,600 in taxes. It is important to remember the effect of having an extra $20,000 growing tax deferred.

If a QDRO is used to order a lump sum to be paid to a former spouse from a defined contribution plan, be sure to notify the plan administrator whether the funds are to be transferred in whole or in part to the intended recipient's separate IRA. This will avoid the 20% income tax withholding that would otherwise be required.

INDIVIDUAL RETIREMENT ACCOUNTS

An Individual Retirement Account (IRA) is not considered a qualified plan, and a rollover may take place without withholding 20% for taxes. In a divorce, IRAs may be transferred in whole or in part. Since an IRA is not a qualified plan, a QDRO is not needed to transfer or divide it. In most cases, the trustee will need to see the judgment for divorce. Check with the trustee to see what they need to transfer or divide the IRA.

You can annuitize an IRA to avoid the 10% penalty by taking substantially equal periodic payments for the longer of five years or until you reach age 59 ½.

DEFINED BENEFIT PLAN

The second major type of retirement plan is the defined benefit plan— frequently referred to as a "pension plan." The parties must determine the value of the participant's interest in the retirement plan. The marital portion generally does not include any portion acquired either before the marriage or after the divorce.

METHODS OF DIVIDING

The courts are struggling with the problem of how to value and divide pensions. To figure out how much of the pension is marital property, you need to know the specifics of the employee's retirement plan.

There are three different methods used to divide pension benefits:

1. **Present value or cash-out method**: The non-employee spouse is paid a lump-sum settlement from the pension or receives a marital asset of equal value to the non-employee spouse's interest in the pension.

2. **Deferred division or future share method**: No present value is determined. Each spouse is awarded a share of the benefits if and when they are paid.

3. **Reserved jurisdiction**: The court retains the authority to order distributions from a pension plan at some point in the future. It should be considered a last resort, as it leaves both spouses in limbo with regard to planning for their future.

A defined benefit retirement plan promises to pay the employee a certain amount per month at retirement time. It has no cash value today.

It can be divided equally or unequally by using a QDRO. If not divided "in kind" later, it must be valued today. This value is placed in the list of marital assets to be offset by other property.

With many pensions, the participant can choose the payout options, such as life, years certain, life of the participant and participant's spouse. The value of a defined benefit plan comes from the company's guarantee to pay based on a predetermined plan formula—not from an account balance.

For instance, the amount of monthly pension could be determined by a complex calculation, which could include:

*   Employee's final average salary

*   An annuity factor based on the employee's age at retirement

*   Employee's annual average Social Security tax base

*   Employee's total number of years of employment and age at retirement

*   Method chosen by the employee to receive payment of voluntary and required contributions

*   Whether a pension will be paid to a survivor upon the employee's death

As you might guess, the valuation of such a plan poses a challenge and has fostered much creativity.

TRANSFERRING ASSETS FROM A DEFINED BENEFIT PLAN

Here is an example of how a defined benefit plan works with Henry and Ginny from the previous example. Assume that based on today's earnings and his length of time with the company, Henry will receive $1,200 a month at age 65 from his pension. He is now age 56, and must wait nine more years before he can start receiving the $1,200 per month. Because of the wait, it is called a "future benefit."

You can, however, value this future stream of income and calculate the present value. The present value should be listed as an asset for purposes of dividing property.

You could, for example, divide the defined benefit plan with a QDRO that states Ginny will receive $600 per month when Henry retires. However, when he retires, his benefit will probably be more than $1,200 per month because he will have additional years of service. When Henry retires, he may get $1,800 a month, but if the QDRO states that Ginny receives $600 per month, she will not get any more even though the value of the fund has increased.

It is important to find out whether the $1,200 per month is what he will get at age 65 based on today's earnings and time with the company, or if the $1,200 per month assumes it is what he will get if he stays with the company until age 65 with projected earnings built in. If it is not clear on the pension statements, these questions must be asked of the plan administrator.

If the couple has less than eight years to wait until retirement, Ginny may choose to wait to get the $600 per month so she can have guaranteed income. However, if Henry is more than eight years away from retirement, she may wish to trade the present value of her share of the pension for another asset. Then Ginny will get the asset now instead of taking a risk with the retirement asset. It is important to consider that many retirement plans have disappeared due to mismanagement of the funds or because companies went out of business.

Assume that Ginny decides to wait for nine years until Henry retires to receive her benefit. They have been married for 32 years. Instead of stating in the QDRO that she will receive $600 per month, it may be more prudent to use a formula (called a coverture fraction), which states that she will receive a percentage of half of the following:

$$\frac{\text{Number of years married while working}}{\text{Total number of years worked until retirement}} = \frac{32}{41}$$

If Henry's final benefit would pay him $1,800 per month:

$$\frac{\left(\frac{32}{41}\right) \times 1{,}800}{2} = 702$$

This may be a more equitable division of the pension based on the premise that Ginny was married to Henry during the early building-up years of the plan.

It is also important to ascertain if the plan will pay Ginny at retirement time (Henry's age 65) in case Henry does not retire at that time. He may decide not to retire just so Ginny cannot get her portion of his retirement plan. Some companies allow the ex-spouse to start receiving benefits at the employee's retirement age even if the employee has not retired. This depends on the retirement plan and the method of dividing the plan pursuant to the QDRO.

CASE STUDIES: THREE DIFFERENT PARAMETERS OF THE DEFINED BENEFIT

Case 1

(The present value is based on leaving the company today.)

Richard will receive $2,600 per month at age 65 from his defined benefit plan, based on his years of service and earnings as of today. He is now age 52. The life expectancy table (see the life expectancy table at the end of the book) shows that he has a life expectancy of an additional 27.11 years. So, his life expectancy right now is 79.11 years. We are going to use 5.5% as the interest rate in all of these examples. However, you should look up the current rates in your practice.

Using the HP12c calculator set your calculator for the beginning of the period (hit the blue button and the 7 key). Input the following data:

PMT	=	2,600	*(monthly payments)*
n	=	169.32	*(number of years between age 65 and 79.11, multiplied by 12 months.)*
i	=	.45833	*(interest rate divided by 12)*
FV	=	0	*(enter 0 for the parameter you are not solving)*

Hit the PV (present value) button.

We find that the PV of the monthly payments is $306,307. That is the amount of money needed at age 65 to be able to pay Richard $2,600 per month for 14.11 years, which is his life expectancy after retirement. Now, calculate the present value as of today:

FV	=	306,307	*(future value)*
n	=	13	*(number of years until he is age 65)*
i	=	5.5	*(interest rate)*
PMT	=	0	*(there are no payments until he retires at age 65)*

Hit the PV (present value) button.

We find that the present value is $152,713. Since there are no payments, calculate using years instead of months. That is the present value today of his future stream of income. It represents the lump sum of money needed today invested at 5.5% to pay Richard $2,600 per month for his life expectancy after retirement. Not all states allow this method of valuation; be sure to check your own state for guidelines and policies.

Case 2

(Based on the same numbers and assumptions as Case 1, but Henry began working for his employer before he was married.)

Henry and Ginny have been married for 15 years, and Henry has worked for his company for 20 years. Therefore, you know only 75% of the present value of his pension is marital property. Henry is now 52, and his life expectancy is 79.11 years. Calculate the present value.

You begin by determining the marital portion of the pension:

$$\left(\frac{15}{20}\right) x \; 152{,}713 = 114{,}534$$

The present value of the marital portion of Henry's pension is $114,534.

Assume you decide to draft the QDRO so that Ginny gets a portion of the monthly payment when Henry retires instead of looking at it as a lump-sum value. In this case, Ginny would be getting half of 75% (37.5%) of $2,600 per month. An order could be entered that awards Ginny $975 per month when Henry reaches age 65.

It might be more financially fair, however, to use the coverture fraction. This is a formula that states the number of Henry's years of plan participation while married to Ginny as the numerator, with the total number of years of plan participation as the denominator.

The calculated lump-sum value of a retirement plan depends on the assumptions you use for the data. There is a lot of litigation surrounding this data because it can make a substantial difference in the present value. Also, some of the discounting assumptions that you make can create a substantial difference.

So, rather than fighting about the value of the pension, you just divide it "in kind." You do not care what the value is because of the percentage division. You could argue that the pension is worth $100,000, so he gets the pension and she gets the $100,000 house. Or, you can just divide the pension 50/50. Again, you do not care if it is worth $150,000, $100,000, or $50,000 because you are dividing it "in kind."

Case 3

(Based on the pension being protected from inflation.)

Marvin is age 52 and plans to retire at age 65. His pension will pay him $2,600 per month based on today's earnings and years of service with the company. We are using the same payments and retirement age so that you can see the difference it makes if there is an inflation-adjusted interest rate. Marvin's pension benefit is protected from inflation and will have a cost of living adjustment each year. The interest rate is 5.5% and the inflation rate is 4%.

To get the inflation-adjusted interest rate, we use the following formula:

$$\frac{1 + discount\ rate}{1 + inflation\ rate} - 1\ x\ 100 = inflation\ adjusted\ interest$$

To find the inflation-adjusted interest rate for Marvin's plan:

$$\frac{1 + 5.5\%}{1 + 4\%} - 1\ x\ 100$$

or:

$$\frac{1.055}{1.04} - 1\ x\ 100 = 1.44$$

Figure the present value of Marvin's pension using the inflation-adjusted interest rate. Again, set your calculator for the beginning of the period (hit the blue button and the 7 key). Input the following data:

PMT	=	2,600	*(monthly payments)*
n	=	169.32	*(number of years between age 65 and 79.11, multiplied by 12 months)*
i	=	.12	*(interest rate divided by 12)*
FV	=	0	*(enter 0 for the parameter you are not solving)*

Hit the PV button.

The present value of the payments at age 65 is $397,819. Of course, this value is higher than Case 1, where the interest rate was not adjusted by inflation.

Between now and Marvin's retirement, we use our regular interest rate because there are no payments that need to be adjusted.

Now, calculate the present value as of today:

FV	=	397,819	*(future value)*
n	=	13	*(number of years until he is age 65)*
i	=	5.5	*(interest rate)*
PMT	=	0	*(there are no payments until he retires at age 65)*

Hit the PV button.

The present value of Marvin's inflation-protected pension is $198,337.

QUALIFIED DOMESTIC RELATIONS ORDER (QDRO)

A QDRO is an order from the court to the retirement plan administrator spelling out how the plan's benefits are to be assigned to each party in a divorce. QDROs should be drafted by professionals who know what they are doing—an attorney or someone who specializes in QDROs.

Plans divisible by a QDRO include defined contribution pension plans, defined benefit pension plans, 401(k)s, thrift savings plans, some profit sharing and money purchase plans, Keogh plans, tax-sheltered annuities, ESOPs, and the old PAYSOPs.

Plans that are not divisible by a QDRO include some plans of small employers not covered by ERISA and many public employee group funds such as police and fire groups and city, state, and other governmental employees including federal employees.

The QDRO is sent to the employer's pension plan administrator. It states how the pension is to be divided between the spouses. This amount can be from zero to 100%, depending on how they have divided the other assets. It does not automatically mean 50%. A phrase often used by attorneys is, "We are going to QDRO that pension," and they are thinking about a 50% split because that is most typical. By definition, however, it does not mean 50%.

Typically, the QDRO not only states how the money in the plan is to be divided, but also what happens to the assets when either party dies.

LEGISLATIVE BACKGROUND

Employee Retirement Income Security Act of 1974 (ERISA)

The enactment of ERISA in 1974 established laws relating to the attachment of pension benefits, thereby putting family law courts into a quandary as to how to treat retirement plan assets that state courts clearly determined were marital property.

Uniformed Services Former Spouses' Protection Act (USFSPA)

The USFSPA was enacted in 1982; it recognizes military retirement benefits as marital property and asserts that a state court may divide them pursuant to state law. A state court may order direct payment of benefits to an ex-spouse, not to exceed one-half of the benefit, if during the marriage the military spouse was in the service for at least ten years.

Retirement Equity Act of 1984 (REA)

The REA of 1984 provides that all qualified plans subject to ERISA may segregate assets for the benefit of an "alternate payee" through a court order known as a qualified domestic relations order (QDRO). Many non-ERISA plans will also honor these orders.

Tax Reform Act of 1984 (TRA)

TRA added Code Sec. 1041, which allows marital property to be transferred back and forth between spouses without creating any tax on the transfer. The income tax basis of each asset is the basis of the asset in the hands of the transferor.

QDRO LIMITATIONS

You must look at the pension documents during the divorce proceedings and before the divorce is final. There are too many horror stories where the case has gone to court, everything is settled, and the judge says the divorce is final and that a QDRO should be drafted to give the ex-spouse her half of the pension as a lump sum. The QDRO is sent to the pension plan and the ex-spouse ends up not getting any of the plan money. Why? Because the plan does not have to pay a lump sum and will not pay any of the benefits to the spouse.

From IBM Pension and Retirement Plan:

Q: "How long does it take for a plan to approve a QDRO?"

A: "The answer and our experience has been that it can take several months. This is because draft orders that have been entered without our advance review often have conditions that we cannot implement or which require forms of payment which are not allowed under the plan. For example, we often see orders that require an immediate lump-sum payment of the former spouse's total share of the benefit. Since the IBM retirement plan does not pay in lump sums except for accrued benefits with a present actuarial value of $3,500 or less or for PRP benefits, but pays only on a monthly basis for life, an order requiring a lump-sum payment must be rejected and will not be accepted until the court has issued an order that complies with the provisions of the plan."[3]

A QDRO generally may not require a plan to provide any form of benefit not otherwise provided under the plan, nor may it require the plan to provide increased benefits. However, within certain limits, it is permissible for a QDRO to require that payments to the alternate payee begin on or after the participant's earliest retirement age, even though the participant has not retired at that time. An area of liability in drafting a QDRO for a pension plan is when the pension documents do not allow for the ex-spouse to receive benefits before the employee spouse has retired.

---

[3] *Informational Guide on "QDROs" Under the IBM Retirement Plan, Prepared for Counsel in Domestic Relations Matters. June 1, 1991.*

An expert from a pension department once said, "We will answer any question that you ask, but we will not volunteer any information." You need to ask the questions. The client does not really understand how to ask questions, and sometimes the attorney does not either. You should at least call the company's pension department and ask:

- Do you allow a QDRO?

- Will you pay it in a lump sum?

- Will you separate the accounts?

- Can the non-employee spouse receive benefits before the employee spouse retires?

Pension departments will not calculate the present value of a pension for you, and you cannot ask specific questions about the client's account unless you have his or her signature that releases such information to you.

PUBLIC EMPLOYEE PENSIONS

Another type of defined benefit plan is for public employees such as schoolteachers, principals, librarians, firemen, policemen, and state troopers. This type of plan typically will not allow any division pursuant to a QDRO, and in some states the plan assets are not assignable at all to the ex-spouse.

Each year, a public employee will get a statement showing his or her contributions to this plan. This sum of money (plus interest) is what the employee can take if he or she quits or is fired. However, if the employee stays in the job for a minimum number of years (usually 20 or 25), he or she will receive an annuity retirement payout that is a percent of his or her final average pay. It is at retirement time that the employee sees the contribution from the public employer.

Janice and Frank had been married for 23 years. Frank began his career as a schoolteacher, and at the time of their divorce, he was the principal of the high school in their small city. His retirement account statement showed that he had paid in $82,050 and Frank used that number as the value of his retirement plan. His attorney accepted this number.

Janice's attorney encouraged her to hire a CDFA professional who determined that when Frank retires, he will get 60% of his final average salary, or $32,050 per year. The financial expert testified in court that the present value of the marital portion of that future stream of income was $373,060—a far cry from $82,050. The judge, after dividing all the other assets equally, declared that Frank still owed Janice $133,585, which should be paid to her via a property settlement note over 15 years at $1,500 per month. Frank's attorney was caught off-guard and now carefully reviews his clients' retirement plans.

DISCOUNT RATE OF INTEREST

To calculate the present value of a future stream of income, there is a relationship between the interest rate and the present value. Fluctuations in the interest rate can have a significant impact on the value of the pension. If you valued the pension long before the divorce was final, then it may be better to recalculate the value of the pension using current rates. As the interest rate increases, the present value will decline, and as the interest rate declines, the value of the pension will increase.

The Pension Benefit Guaranty Corporation (PBGC), which is a federal corporation, announces the monthly interest rates for the following month. The rate that is used to calculate the present value of pension plans is based on average annuity rates. This has become the reliable national standard for computing present values of pensions in divorce cases because it removes doubt and speculation of battling experts regarding the interest rate. Look at your state law to determine which rate to use. You can look at the interest rate table at the PBGC website, www.pbgc.gov.

The PBGC has changed its whole structure of calculating interest rates to better conform to GATT (General Agreement on Tariffs and Trade). Many plans are required to use the PBGC lump-sum rate to calculate the interest. The plan cannot use the GATT rate unless the plan is amended to allow that.

The GATT mandated that by the year 2000, all qualified plans had to amend their plan documents to use the GATT rate when figuring the present value of pensions. The GATT rate is the previous 30-day average of 30-year treasuries.

Calculating the GATT rate has become increasingly difficult, if not impossible, because the government is no longer selling the 30-year bond. One possible solution would be to use the 30-year T-Bond index, which is a market-driven rate and is used in trade around the world. For a quote, enter the symbol TYX (the security type would be indices) into the stock quote service that you use and then divide the quote by 10 for the actual rate.

In many states, the present value of a pension plan must be calculated by using the earliest date of retirement that can be taken without a penalty or reduction of benefits. Before this rule was established, one expert would say, "This is the value of his pension when he retires at age 65." The other expert would say, "But he is going to take early retirement at age 55 so this is the value of his pension instead." Obviously, two different values would be produced. For example, if a company allows retirement at the age of 60 with full benefits, figure the present value from that age. Make sure you verify which method is used in your jurisdiction.

Death Watch Out!

Look

SURVIVOR BENEFITS

It is critical to work with the plan administrator to set up the survivor benefits when a defined benefit plan is divided between the spouses. Your client would be very unhappy if she was supposed to get 50% of the defined benefit plan, but upon the death of her ex-husband, the plan administrator refused to pay any additional money from the plan.

The QDRO needs to state simplistically whether the spouses are taking the joint and survivor annuity option, which, of course, will reduce their ultimate benefit.

Another option for the non-participant spouse is to have his or her portion (i.e., 50%) set up as a separate account. Then the payment will be calculated and annuitized at the time of payment. With either of these two options the non-participant gets their portion whether the employee dies or not.

Make sure that you understand the plan and that there are options available in the event of the death of the employee and that you have included them in your planning.

With a QDRO, an ex-wife can preserve her right to receive survivor's benefits if her husband dies before he retires. This means that an ex-husband must obtain his ex-wife's written consent (and have it notarized) to waive her rights to the survivor's benefits—even if he has remarried and wants his new spouse to receive the benefits instead. A divorce decree that earmarks the money for a former spouse can override the rights of a second or third spouse.

VESTING

As discussed earlier in this chapter, a participant is vested when he or she has an immediate, fixed right to the present or future enjoyment of an accrued benefit. The percentage of vesting is the portion that the employee is entitled to from the retirement plan when he or she retires, quits, or is fired.

When "fully vested," an employee is entitled to all of the benefits that the employer has contributed. Being "partially vested" means that if the employee quit his or her job, he or she would be able to take only a specified percentage of the employer's contributions. An example would be if the employee were 40% vested and the employer's contributions were $1,500, the employee could take $600.

Any contributions made by the employee to the plan are immediately 100% vested. The employee is always entitled to take all of his or her contributions plus the earnings on those contributions.

An employee must be given a non-forfeitable right to his accrued benefits from employer contributions in accordance with one of the following two vesting schedules:

- **5-year cliff vesting:** An employee who has at least five years of service must have a non-forfeitable right to 100% of the employee's accrued benefit [IRC §411(a)(2)(A)].

- **3- to 7-year vesting (7 year graded vesting):** An employee who has completed at least three years of service must have a non-forfeitable right to at least the following percentages of his or her accrued benefit: 20% after three years of service, 40% after four years of service, 60% after five years of service, 80% after six years of service, and 100% after seven years of service [IRC §411(a)(2)(B)].

Top-heavy plans or matching contributions typically use 3 year cliff vesting or 6 year graded vesting.

It is important to find out whether the state considers non-vested retirement benefits to be marital property. If so, a defined contribution plan's total value could be divided, and the employee could leave his job and never receive the non-vested amount.

For example, Marvin worked for ABC, Inc. His 401(k) was worth $58,000, which was made up of $12,300 from his contributions and $45,700 from his employer's contributions. Marvin is 40% vested. If he quit his job today, he could take his contributions of $12,300 and $18,280 of his employer's contributions for a total of $30,580. He and his ex-wife Susie agreed to value his 401(k) at the full $58,000 for purposes of dividing property. Marvin kept his 401(k) and paid Susie $29,000 for her half out of the savings account money. Six months after the divorce was final, ABC, Inc. laid off half its workforce— including Marvin. He left the company with $30,580 from his retirement account. The net result was that he ended up $13,710 short after the division of marital property.

MATURE PLANS

An employee may be fully vested but may still have to wait until he or she reaches a certain age before being able to receive any benefits. For instance, some companies do not pay out benefits until the employee has reached age 60 or age 65. In some cases, if the employee is not vested in the plan and dies before retirement age, the benefits are lost. Nobody gets them.

DOUBLE DIPPING

Sometimes, a retirement plan is divided as part of the property division. In some states, when the employee retires, the income from his portion of the retirement plan is taken into

DAVE Read! When did you and Chris plan on Retiring

consideration to calculate spousal and child support. The end result is that the non-employee spouse is getting paid twice from the same asset.

THE CARROT STORY

Understanding how defined benefit pensions really work is often confusing to even the most knowledgeable financial experts. The following excerpt from *Assigning Retirement Benefits In Divorce* by Gale S. Finley is an excellent and delightful way to learn and comprehend the ins and outs of defined benefit plans.[4]

Imagine a farm in central Kentucky that raises racehorses. The owner of the farm takes his racing very seriously and comes up with way to reward his horses for winning races for him. He calls it the "Carrot Retirement Plan." He decides that after each horse retires from racing, it will be provided an allocation of carrots each week as a supplement to its regular diet. The number of carrots a horse receives each week depends upon the number of races it wins during its racing career.

Each horse will receive its weekly allotment of carrots until it goes to that big pasture in the sky.

In order to ensure an adequate supply of carrots for his retiring horses, the owner decides to plan ahead and start growing and freezing carrots. He sits down with the veterinarian and the two of them decide how many carrots he will have to grow and store each week.

They look at how many horses he has, how many races each has won, when each is expected to retire, and how long each is expected to live after retirement. Based upon those initial projections, the owner comes up with a quantity of carrots that will be needed to be planted that first year. He hires an expert in carrot growing – the Keeper of the Carrots – to maintain a carrot crop that will continue to produce an adequate supply to meet future carrot obligations.

The next year the owner again sits down with his veterinarian and the Keeper of the Carrots. The owner and the veterinarian discuss factors bearing on the number of carrots that will be needed for all the retiring horses down the road, such as any new horses acquired during the year, any that have died during the year, how many races each has won, and how many will be retiring. Also, they reevaluate their projections from the previous year concerning all those same factors based upon what actually occurred during the year. The Keeper of the Carrots then reports on how well the carrot crop came in during the year and whether it will be adequate given the number of carrots the owner

---

[4] Assigning Retirement Benefits in Divorce, A Practical Guide to Negotiating and Drafting QDROs. *Gale S. Finley, pages 17-21, American Bar Association, 1995.*

has projected under the Carrot Retirement Plan. They also discuss the number of carrots that will have to be planted during the next year.

One of the horses covered under the Carrot Retirement Plan is the "Participant Horse." This Participant Horse is still actively racing and occasionally winning. In addition, he has won enough races through today's date to be entitled to receive 10 carrots each week of his life beginning on the date he is permanently turned out to pasture (its "Accrued Carrot Benefit"). What can we say about this horse's rights under the Carrot Retirement Plan as of today's date? What the Participant Horse has today is a right to receive 10 carrots each week for life beginning at some future date. If he wins more races in the future, the number of weekly carrots to which he is entitled will increase. But as of today, 10 per week is the number. Remember though, it is a current right to receive carrots in the future if the Participant Horse lives long enough to receive them. The Participant Horse does not "own" any carrots. Because he is still racing, he is not currently entitled to any carrots. In fact, because he may die before he retires, he may never receive any carrots.

The owner of the horse farm owns thousands of carrots that are being stored to someday give the Participant Horse and all his co-retirees a certain number of carrots each week for their respective lives. But the Participant Horse does not own any carrots until he actually receives his first weekly allotment.

Assuming another horse – the "A-P Horse" – wants to lay claim to 50% of the Participant Horse's Accrued Carrot Benefit, what do we have to divide? We have the Participant Horse's right to receive 10 carrots per week for his life beginning when he retires. We can split that down the middle so that the A-P Horse will get five carrots from each 10 carrot allotment as it is distributed to the Participant Horse during his lifetime. That is the easiest way to make the division because the number of carrots to be given, the beginning date, and the ending date are already determined. No muss and no fuss.

As simple as that method may be, however, it means that the A-P Horse has absolutely no control over any aspect of the carrot distribution process. The A-P Horse may want to start receiving her carrots sooner or later than the Participant Horse's retirement date. The A-P Horse may want the security of knowing the carrots will keep coming during her lifetime rather than the lifetime of the Participant Horse (rumor has it the Participant Horse's health is deteriorating). Can we simply provide that the A-P Horse will receive five carrots each week during her life, beginning when she chooses? We cannot if our goal is to give the A-P Horse a right to only 50% of the Participant Horse's Accrued Carrot Benefit as of today's date.

To understand that, look at the Participant Horse's Accrued Carrot Benefit. We will assume that the Participant Horse will retire in two years and will start receiving 10 carrots each week beginning November 1 of that year. At that time the Participant Horse will have a life expectancy of 20 years. If these assumptions hold true, the owner will need to be prepared to provide 10,400 carrots (10 carrots x 52 weeks x 20 years) to the Participant Horse over his lifetime. If we assume a 50/50 split of the carrots, the Participant Horse receives only five carrots per week, and the lifetime total becomes 5,200 carrots.

Now assume that A-P Horse, because of an age difference, has a current life expectancy of 24 years. If the A-P Horse starts to receive five carrots per week (based upon the 50% assignment) starting now (assuming this is the "earliest retirement age") and continuing for the assumed 24 years, she will receive an aggregate of 6,240 carrots over her lifetime. This is substantially more than 50% of the Accrued Carrot Benefit or 5,200 carrots. Moreover, when added to the 5,200 the owner expects to give to the Participant Horse, the total (11,440) is significantly higher than the 10,400 that would be given (if all assumptions are accurate) to the Participant Horse if no assignment is made. Since the owner is only obligated to give out 10,400 carrots under the Carrot Retirement Plan, something has to change.

If, in fact, the intent of the parties is to give the A-P Horse during her lifetime the equivalent of 5,200 carrots over the lifetime of the Participant Horse, a couple of options exist. As we mentioned earlier, the A-P Horse can receive half of the Participant Horse's weekly allotment of carrots while the Participant horse is alive. But to keep carrots coming to the A-P Horse after the Participant Horse dies, she can also require the Carrot Retirement Plan to continue to deliver to her the same weekly allotment. Of course, in order to "fund" her continuing carrot supply after the death of the Participant Horse, the Carrot Retirement Plan will need to reduce the number of weekly carrots that are given out while the Participant Horse is alive. For example, upon the death of the Participant Horse, it would be incorrect to continue to give 10 carrots per week to the A-P Horse (five that would have been given to the Participant Horse and five to the A-P Horse, who is expected to live longer than the Participant Horse).

Another option is for the A-P Horse to be treated as though she has her own Accrued Carrot Benefit. She would receive fewer carrots per week beginning when she chooses and continuing for as long as she lives. In our example, the latter option would result in the A-P Horse immediately beginning to receive 4.17 (5200 divided by 24 years divided by 52 weeks) per week for her lifetime.

Either of these two options will provide the A-P Horse with 50% of the Participant Horse's Accrued Carrot Benefit. If the life expectancy assumptions for the Participant Horse and the A-P Horse hold true, both Horses will end up with the same aggregate number of carrots that the Participant Horse would have received during his life if the carrots were not divided.

THE PITFALLS OF DIVIDING PENSIONS

The improper division of pensions can subject the professionals involved to grievances and lawsuits for malpractice. Being aware of the pitfalls of dividing retirement plans and taking appropriate precautionary action will avoid such unpleasant claims.

According to Robert C. Treat, JD, an expert on QDROs, the main problem areas regarding division of retirement plans are: timeliness, a failure to address key issues, and an incomplete understanding of the process (on the part of the professional and/or the clients).[5] Let's take a closer look at these potential pitfalls.

- **The QDROs must be timely.**

    - Many times the QDRO is an afterthought even though it is the mechanism by which one of the largest assets is divided. Unfortunately, this sometimes means the QDRO is delayed, or even forgotten. This is the single worst pitfall. If the participant dies or remarries and retires with a different beneficiary than the would-be alternate payee (his or her former spouse), then it is usually too late to assign the benefits to the former spouse. Often, the divorcing parties think the divorce decree has it covered, so there is nothing to remind the person who is responsible for drafting and processing the QDRO to get it done—and years can go by before the alternate payee realizes his or her benefits are not being paid as they should. At that point, everyone realizes there is a very, very big problem.

    - Consider the case where the participant dies the day after the parties are divorced, but the QDRO hasn't been done. In pensions, the default form of payment for a single person is a life-only benefit, and under these circumstances, the plan administrator might effectively argue that the disposition of the participant's benefit has been determined, and that since the form of benefit is a life-only annuity for the participant's lifetime, there are no benefits payable whatsoever, to anyone. Because of this particular fact pattern, the QDRO should be drafted before the parties are divorced and entered in court concurrently with the divorce

---

[5] *Robert C. Treat, Jr. (JD) runs QDRO Express, a business that prepares QDROs for attorneys and provides other divorce litigation support in the area of retirement plans. He is licensed to practice law in Michigan, and is an active member of the QDRO Committee for the Family Law Section of the State of Michigan Bar Association. He has prepared thousands of QDROs, testified as an expert witness numerous times in the area of QDROs and retirement plans, written numerous articles on the topic for the Michigan Family Law Journal, authored the section of the State of Michigan's Institute of Continuing Legal Education's publication "QDROs, EDROs & Division of Employee Benefits on Divorce" dealing with division of IRAs and federal pensions, testified before the State of Michigan Senate Judiciary committee regarding legislation to improve how retirement plans are divided, assisted in the drafting of such legislation, and he speaks publicly on the topic of QDROs to professionals in Michigan and across the country.*

decree.

- **The QDRO must be drafted correctly.**

  - **Failure to address an issue**

    - ERISA Section 206(d)(3)(C)(i)-(iv) and IRC §414(p)(2)(A)-(D) require the QDRO to contain the last known mailing address of both parties, the correct formal name of each plan to which the order applies, sufficient instruction to determine the amount of the benefit, and the number of payments or time period to which the order applies. The number one reason that plan administrators reject the first attempted QDRO is that the plan name is incorrect, followed closely by unclear or omitted provisions in the QDRO.

    - The drafter should address what happens at the death of the alternate payee, not just the death of the participant—does the benefit revert to the participant, go to the alternate payee's beneficiary, or simply cease.

    - Early retirement supplements and post-retirement cost-of-living adjustments should be addressed unless the defaults for the plan meet the intent of the parties, and even then, an affirmative statement as to whether such benefits are awarded, and in what amounts, is preferred to a document that is silent regarding such benefits.

    - For defined contribution plans, the issues of outstanding loans, earnings on the awarded amount, and contributions made after the date of division but attributable to periods prior to such date should be clearly spelled out in the QDRO.

  - **Failure to define a term or the amount of a particular benefit**

    - The term "marital portion" is not self-explanatory. The plan needs clear instruction as to how to calculate the marital portion. For defined benefit plans, the methods can be the subtraction method, accrued coverture, and prospective coverture. For defined contribution plans, the drafter should specify—either expressly or implicitly—whether earnings on premarital amounts are to be divided.

    - The plan also needs clear instruction as to the amount of the survivor benefit to be paid to the alternate payee, if any. This can be the entire benefit, the marital portion, the same amount the alternate payee would have received had the participant lived and retired voluntarily, or some other amount.

  - **Failure to properly coordinate the awarded benefits**

    - You must understand the benefits of the plan. Always obtain and read a summary plan description and whatever materials the plan provides to assist QDRO drafters and divorcing parties. Call the plan administrator if you are uncertain about how the benefits work.

- Survivor benefits are the most difficult part of QDRO drafting because they are the least understood.

  - An award based on the lifetime of the alternate payee does not generally require a post-retirement survivor annuity because it will last for the alternate payee's lifetime—but an award based on the lifetime of the participant generally does require a post-retirement survivor annuity because the alternate payee's pension benefits would cease upon the participant's death.

  - If a participant is remarried at retirement, the new spouse gets all the survivor benefits unless the QDRO provides for survivor benefits for the alternate payee (former spouse).

  - If the participant is single at retirement, the normal form of benefit is generally a single life annuity for the participant's lifetime, so it is important to get the QDRO implemented by the plan before the participant retires, as the QDRO can specify that the form of benefit shall provide for a survivor annuity.

- Some plans do not allow an award of cost of living adjustments and/or early retirement supplements if the portion of the accrued benefit awarded to the alternate payee is based on the lifetime of the alternate payee.

- Most defined benefit plans and a few defined contribution plans do not allow the alternate payee to receive benefits until the participant's earliest retirement age under the plan. This can be an unpleasant surprise if the alternate payee is counting on an immediate distribution to cover the cost of the divorce or other cash needs.

- Some plans offer early retirement buyouts, windows, or incentives, and some plans will not allow such benefits to be assigned by QDRO, even if they are benefits that are paid from the plan itself. Thus, the QDRO should address these benefits if divisible by QDRO, and if they cannot be divided by QDRO, the parties should be advised that some other agreement must be made if the benefits are to be divided.

- **Failure to understand the QDRO process and failure to adequately inform the parties about it**

  - After the divorce is final is not the time to inform the parties that they will need QDROs and that the process will take from a few weeks to a few months, maybe more. The parties are usually expecting—and even hoping—that their dealings with each other are complete at this point.

- The parties should be informed early on that QDROs will be necessary, and that they will need to maintain the attorney-client relationship until the process is complete. They should understand that research will be necessary, and that many draft QDROs are rejected on the first attempt, but that the drafter will send the draft QDROs for conditional preapproval if the plan allows. They should be informed that the drafter will send the QDROs to the attorneys, who will review them for accuracy and to ensure the intent is met and who will obtain all the signatures and enter the QDROs in court and send them to the plan administrators. They should not expect this process to take less than two or three months, no matter how quickly the drafter works.

In conclusion, the above are the most common areas that give angst to the parties and the professionals helping them. Be advised that government retirement plans have different rules than ERISA plans, and even within the public and private sectors, similar retirement plans can differ greatly in the benefits provided and in plan policy as to QDROs. The above is not an exhaustive discussion of how to draft QDROs; formal training, independent research, and reading are also required to become competent in this area.

CHAPTER 3
THE MARITAL HOME

Learning Objectives

After completing this chapter, you will be able to:

1. State the different options for the marital home.
2. Calculate the cost basis and the capital gain on the sale of the home.
3. Explain tax issues on the sale of the principal residence, including "use period" and "ownership period" (special rules relating to divorce).
4. Recognize the financial viability of one spouse keeping the residence.

In many divorces, the biggest question is who gets the marital home. Should the wife get it, should the husband, or should they sell it and split the proceeds? What if the house is "underwater," meaning that the homeowners owe more on their mortgages than their houses are worth? The answer is not always easy or clear.

In a normal economy, couples typically build equity in their homes; if they decide to divorce, they would usually divide the equity they built by selling the house or by one partner buying out the other's share. But after the recent boom-and-bust cycle, many couples own houses that neither spouse can afford to maintain individually, and that they cannot sell for what they owe. CoreLogic[6], a leading provider of financial and property information and services to business and government, has calculated that more than 5.3 million homes—or 10.7% of all mortgaged properties—had negative equity in 2014. Nevada (26%), Florida (24%), and Arizona (19%) were the top three states where mortgaged properties have negative equity.

Let's look at a few possibilities for dividing the marital home when it has negative equity. We will use the following fact pattern to illustrate the options:

Anne and James purchased a home in 2007; the current mortgage value is $237,000. The house was recently appraised at $192,000, and there are several similar houses for sale or in foreclosure in their subdivision. In addition to the home, they have a savings account with $97,000, credit card debt of $12,000, Anne's 403(b) plan with $30,000, and his IRA with $50,000. This year, they decided to divorce. Anne asked to remain in the house with their three-year-old son, and James would like to accommodate her request.

---

[6] *To see CoreLogic's research, go to www.corelogic.com and click on the "Insights" button.*

Anne and James have considered the following options:

1. **Keep the house.**

    - Anne could contact the lender regarding modification of the existing mortgage under the HARP program. The HARP program is available for mortgages guaranteed by Fannie Mae or Freddie Mac. (www.makinghomeaffordable.gov), and the FHA Short Refinance is available for those mortgages not guaranteed by Fannie Mae, Freddie Mac, FHA, VA, or USDA. These programs are designed to reduce the mortgage payment and sometimes the deficiency to allow an individual to retain the home. Anne would have to apply and qualify for the mortgage. This solution would also serve to remove James from the mortgage.

    - Anne could remain in the house and keep the current mortgage. She and James could agree to include a provision in their settlement agreement that reserves the court's jurisdiction to divide and award the house for a certain period of time. They could divide the remainder of the marital property while continuing to hold some assets and/or debts outstanding – waiting for conditions to improve prior to division. For example, Anne and James could agree to divide the bank account equally, reserving jurisdiction over the division and/or allocation of the house and the mortgage. They could then wait for the house's value to increase sufficiently to either break even on a sale of the home – or even profit from it.

    - To ensure an equal overall division, Anne and James could also agree that James would receive the credit card debt, his IRA, and $22,000 of the savings account. Anne would receive $75,000 of the saving account and her 403(b). She is getting the lion's share of the savings and no credit card debt because she is also receiving the mortgage on the home – which exceeds the value by $43,000.

2. **Sell the house.**

    - Anne and James could approach the lender to arrange a short sale, which would eliminate the deficiency and let Anne and James walk away without any debt associated with the house. However, it would mean that both would need to find and move to new residences.

    - Anne and James could also choose to sell the house and simply pay off the deficiency from their savings and retirement accounts. Let's consider a slight change in the fact pattern: the balance in the savings account is now $22,000, James has $145,000 in a 401(k) plan (rather than an IRA). Anne could receive $75,000 from James's 401(k) and use $43,000 to pay off the deficiency. As long as the funds are taken from James's qualified account and used to pay the deficiency—and not deposited into an IRA for Anne—the funds are not subject to the early withdrawal penalty. See Internal Revenue Code Section 72(t)(2)(C) for more information.

- Finally, the couple could choose to allow the home to go into foreclosure. During the foreclosure period, no mortgage payments are made and money can be put aside for new housing.

In reviewing their options, it is important to consider whether the couple is in an equitable distribution or a community property state. In a community property state, the couple may be required to provide documentation that they have agreed to an unequal division of property due to the negative equity on the house. It is also important to remember that a foreclosure does not erase the deficiency, and that the mortgage company can come after either party to receive payment on the remaining balance.

Many times, one spouse has an emotional tie to the home and wants to keep it. Unfortunately, he or she may not think about the value of the asset. If it is almost paid off and has a lot of equity, he or she is getting an illiquid asset that does not buy groceries or create any income.

OPTIONS

There are generally three options for the home: sell the home, have one spouse buy out the other spouse's interest, or have both spouses continue to own the home.

Sell the Home

Selling the home and dividing the proceeds is the easiest and cleanest way to divide the equity in the home. Concerns that need to be addressed include the basis and possible capital gains, buying another home versus renting, and being able to qualify for a new loan.

Buy Out the Other Spouse

Buying out the other spouse's interest works if one person wants to remain in the home or wants to own the home, but there are difficulties with this option that should be considered.

First, the value of the home needs to be agreed upon to determine the equity in the home. Next, decide on the dollar amount of the buyout. Will the buyout amount be reduced by projected selling costs and possible capital gains taxes (in case the owner needs to sell it sooner than expected)?

There may be other assets that can be transferred to the spouse who surrenders the home. If there are inadequate assets, another means to pay for the home must be selected. The home could be refinanced to withdraw cash to pay off the other spouse or a note payable can be drawn up with terms of payment agreeable to both parties. In the case of a note, reasonable interest should be charged and it should be collateralized with a deed of trust on the property.

A problem with this arrangement is that it keeps the ex-spouses in an uncomfortable debtor-creditor relationship.

There is another problem with buying out the other spouse's interest. Let's say the wife wants the home and both names are on the deed. The husband can transfer the home by quitclaim deed to her so that only her name is on the title. Then she can sell the home at any time. Although his name is off the deed, it remains on the mortgage. He is still liable if she decides to quit making the payments. The mortgage company may not care if they are divorced, and will probably refuse to "release" the other spouse. The only way he can get his name off the mortgage may be for her to assume the loan, refinance it, or pay it off. When the husband's name is kept on the mortgage, this may impact his credit. He could be viewed as overextended unless he has proof that she is making the mortgage payments. If they have an adversarial relationship, this could cause additional problems.

Joint Ownership of the Home

The final option is to continue owning the property jointly. This is generally an option for couples that want their children to stay in the same home until they finish school, reach a certain age, or the resident ex-spouse remarries or cohabits. The couple usually agrees to sell the home and divide the proceeds after the children have graduated from school or after another contingency occurs.

The most logical way to split the expenses would be for both spouses to pay half of the mortgage payments and all improvements and major repairs. Improvements and major repairs should be split, since they would increase or maintain the value of the asset; they also increase the cost basis of the home. Property taxes, utilities, minor repairs, and insurance should probably be paid by the resident spouse; minor repairs increase neither the value nor the cost basis of the home. If the property taxes or mortgage payments are paid by only one spouse after the divorce is final, then the payor spouse can only deduct his or her half of the payments and the non-payor spouse would not be able to take any deductions. Again, this creates a tie between the ex-spouses that may create additional stress.

To help put all these options into perspective, here are some examples. Mark and Susan both had very good jobs when they decided to divorce in 2006. Susan wanted to stay in the home with their three children and buy out Mark's half of the home with a property settlement note. The note was signed when interest rates were higher, and she agreed to pay him his half of the equity at 7% interest. Then property values began to decline. Susan's half of the equity was losing value, and his half was earning 7% – even after the interest rates plummeted.

Nobody presumed at the time they drew up this agreement that interest rates or property values were going to go down. There are always risks when agreements extend into the future. These risks can run both ways.

Lila and Keith divided all of their property and she owed him $5,000. Lila kept the home, which she planned to sell in three years when their daughter was out of high school. The home had $20,000 of equity in it at the time of divorce. They both agreed that when she sold the home in three years, she would give him his $5,000. However, Lila's attorney knew Susan's lawyer and heard that Susan was paying 7% interest. Lila's attorney suggested, "Since $5,000 represents 25% of the equity, why don't you agree on a percentage? That way, when you sell your home you give him 25% of the proceeds. If your home declines in value and there is only a $10,000 profit, you are not paying him half. Or if it goes up, you both win because you both get more."

If you are talking about dividing assets within the next year, consider specifying an exact dollar amount. Beyond a year, the amount should be specified as a percentage of the proceeds from the sale of the home.

Cost Basis

June and Stan are getting divorced and they have three assets: a hunting cabin on a lake valued at $190,000, a 401(k) plan valued at $90,000, and a certificate of deposit (CD) for $140,000.

Stan said, "Why don't you take the cabin and sell it?" He had borrowed $140,000 against the cabin a year before and put that money into the CD. "If you sell it, you will get $50,000. You take the 401(k) worth $90,000, and I'll take the CD, so we'll each end up with $140,000." June talked this over with her attorney and they thought this sounded fair.

	Assets	June	Stan
Cabin	$190,000		
Mortgage	(140,000)		
Equity	50,000	$50,000	
401(k)	90,000	90,000	
CD	$140,000		$140,000
Total	**$280,000**	**$140,000**	**$140,000**

What Stan did not mention—and what the attorney should have considered—was the basis in the cabin. Stan paid $20,000 for this cabin 15 years earlier. The sale of the cabin generates $170,000 in capital gains, which creates a tax of $34,000 (capital gains tax of 15% plus state tax of 5%). June received $50,000 and had to pay $34,000 in taxes, so she ended up with only $16,000.

Capital gain	$170,000
Federal tax (15%)	25,500
State tax (5%)	8,500
Total tax	**$34,000**

In addition, the after-tax value (federal and state) of the 401(k) plan is approximately $60,000. So June's share of the assets is valued at only $76,000. Meanwhile, Stan walks away with his CD worth $140,000 tax-free.

Stan ends up with $140,000 and June ends up with $76,000 because June's attorney never considered the cost basis of the cabin or the taxes upon distribution of the 401(k). Do you think June's attorney had some liability here? Absolutely!

	Assets	**June**	**Stan**
Cabin	$16,000	$16,000	
401(k)	60,000	60,000	
CD	140,000		$140,000
Total	**$216,000**	**$76,000**	**$140,000**

We find that the one question most overlooked by attorneys is: "What is the basis of the home (or stocks, other real estate, or other investments)?"

NOTE: If improvements are made to a house they are added to the basis. The cost of repairs does not increase the basis of property.

TAX ISSUES – SALE OF THE PRINCIPAL RESIDENCE

Since the Tax Relief Act of 1997 (TRA '97), many taxpayers have not had to pay capital gain taxes on the sale of their principal residence, and those in regions with higher property values have had their tax burden reduced. More recent tax law changes have reduced the capital gains tax to 15% for most taxpayers. Taxpayers can exclude a certain dollar amount of capital gains from tax when they sell their principal residence. The amount that can be excluded depends on their filing status, and they must meet all of the requirements.

The rules are as follows:

• Single taxpayers can exclude $250,000 from capital gains.

• Married taxpayers filing a joint return can exclude $500,000 from capital gains.

• The exclusion is allowed for one sale every two years. There are exceptions to the two-year rule; these include: change in place of employment, health, or unforeseen circumstances.

- Taxpayer(s) must own and use their principal residence for two of the last five years prior to the sale. The two years do not need to be consecutive [IRC §121].

For 2015, the capital gain tax rates are:

- 0% for taxpayers in the 10% or 15% income tax bracket

- 15% for taxpayers in income tax brackets from 25% to 35%

- 20% for taxpayers in the 39.6% bracket

There are special use and ownership rules relating to divorce:

- **Use Period**. If one spouse, pursuant to a divorce decree or separation agreement, is required to grant the other spouse the right to temporary possession of the residence, but retains title to the residence, and it is later sold, the non-occupying spouse will be treated as having used the residence for the period of time that the occupying spouse used the residence.

- **Ownership Period**. If one spouse transfers a residence to the other spouse pursuant to a divorce decree, the "receiving spouse" shall be able to include the "transferring spouse's" ownership period in computing their ownership period. If one spouse remarries prior to the sale of the jointly-owned residence, the remarried spouse can use the new spouse's time to meet the ownership requirements.

Let's look at a couple of examples.

Example 1

John and Mary are getting divorced. John is awarded use of the jointly-owned family residence for four years. At the end of four years, John sells the residence and 50% of the proceeds are sent to Mary.

- **Scenario A:** John sells the residence for $400,000. Mary will receive $200,000 and be entitled to use her $250,000 exclusion even though she has not lived in the residence for the previous four years. She will not owe any tax.

- **Scenario B**: John sells the house for $750,000. Mary's portion of the cost basis is $45,000, and her portion of the selling expenses is $5,000. Mary's half of the mortgage is $70,000. The cost basis and selling expenses are subtracted from the sales price to determine the amount of gain. Even though Mary qualifies for the $250,000 exclusion, she will be taxed on $75,000 of gain. Any mortgage balance has no effect on gain or loss. Mary will receive $375,000 less her share of the selling expenses ($5,000) and her share of the mortgage balance ($70,000) or $300,000.

Sales price	$750,000
Basis	90,000
Selling expenses	10,000
Capital gain	$650,000

Mary's half of sales price	$375,000
Mary's half of basis	45,000
Mary's half of selling expenses	5,000
Mary's half of capital gain	325,000
Mary's exclusion	− 250,000
Mary's taxable capital gain	$75,000

But the new rule is not always advantageous. Let's look at the case of Vicki and Adam.

Example 2

Vicki and Adam are getting divorced and Vicki is taking the house worth $750,000. The basis in the house is $185,000, and her selling expenses are $15,000. Vicki decides to sell her house, move to another city, and buy another house. Her gain on the sale is $550,000. She will be able to use her $250,000 exclusion, but will still have to pay taxes on the remainder of $300,000.

Sales price	$750,000
Basis	185,000
Selling expenses	15,000
Capital gain	$550,000
Exclusion	− 250,000
Taxable amount	$300,000

You can use this exclusion every two years.

Prior to TRA '97, the tax code provided:

- Any gain on the sale of a residence could be rolled over into a new residence of equal or greater value without recognizing any capital gains.

- Taxpayers could use a one-time $125,000 exclusion from capital gain at age 55 or older.

- Capital gains were taxed at 28%.

FINANCIAL VIABILITY OF KEEPING THE RESIDENCE

When Should a Non-Working Spouse Keep the Residence?

There are cases when the non-working (or lower wage-earning) spouse should keep the residence – even when doing so will create an unequal settlement. Let's look at Bill and Barbara.

Bill and Barbara are 45 and 49, respectively, and have been married for 18 years. They have one son. Bill earns $2,175 per month minus child support payments of $413. His living expenses are $1,400 per month, which leaves him with a surplus of $362 per month. Barbara earns $780 per month plus $413 from child support. Her living expenses with her son are $1,630 per month, which creates a negative cash flow of $437 per month.

	Barbara	Bill
Take-home pay	$780	$2,175
Child support	413	(413)
Living expenses	(1,630)	(1,400)
Cash flow	**($437)**	**$362**

The judge decided the assets would be divided as follows:

- Barbara will receive the house, which has equity of $44,000 and her IRA worth $5,000.

- Bill will get his IRA worth $8,900.

- There are no other assets.

- Since Barbara gets the house with $44,000 worth of equity, she has to pay Bill half of that equity upon the first of the following events: if she sells the house, if she remarries, or upon the emancipation of their son.

We do not know if she is going to sell the house or remarry, but we do know that their son is going to reach the age of emancipation within two years. Barbara's house payment is $290 per month with 10 years left on the mortgage. According to this scenario, Barbara is heading for poverty from the outset. To be able to pay Bill his half of the equity in the house, she will have to sell the house. This will force her to rent at a much higher cost than her house payment of $290 per month. In her area, rental prices start at $400 to 450 per month.

This court order is forcing Barbara into severe poverty. In this case, it seems reasonable that Barbara should be allowed to keep the house without paying Bill half the equity – an unequal but equitable settlement.

When the Non-Working Spouse Should Not Keep the Residence

Please refer to the revisions that start on page 56.

The following example illustrates that there are cases when the non-working (or lower wage-earning) spouse cannot afford to keep the family home. The example of Bob and Cindy illustrates, in detail, the financial pitfalls that can arise.

Cindy needs three more years of school to finish college and then she will be able to earn approximately $35,000. Her take-home pay will be $29,194 per year. She will not be able to earn income while she is finishing school. Bob is offering to help Cindy through school by paying spousal support of $2,000 per month for one year, then $1,500 per month for two additional years.

Cindy's expenses with the two children are $51,742 per year. This includes her expenses for school, which average $350 per month. Bob earns $75,000 per year and brings home $57,570 per year. His expenses are $2,050 per month ($24,600 per year).

The family residence has a fair market value (FMV) of $220,000 with a mortgage of $130,000 at 6.5% interest for 15 years. Payments are $1,500 per month (principal, interest, taxes, and insurance). Cindy wants to remain in the residence with the children.

They have a rental house worth $90,000 with a mortgage of $50,000. They are putting the rental up for sale and figure the proceeds after paying the expenses would net them $33,700. That is why the anticipated proceeds are entered as cash instead of as real property. The rental income and expenses are a wash. So, other than the proceeds from the sale of the rental, there is no impact on their cash flow.

Their IRAs total $17,000. They have credit card debt totaling $22,600.

Bob has made the following proposal (called "Scenario 1"). Cindy will take the house, the rental, the IRAs, and the debt. Bob will keep only his business.

Bob feels that since his business is so new and cannot be counted on, he is making a very generous proposal if he takes his business and gives Cindy all of the other property (including the debt).

This couple had trouble staying within their budget during their marriage. Cindy tended to overspend and thus increased their credit card debt. The challenge in this case will be counseling Cindy on the importance of staying within her budget.

Look at the asset table on page 57. The net equity in the house, $90,000, and the net proceeds from the sale of the rental property, $33,700, are in Cindy's column. The IRAs and the debt are also in Cindy's column. The business is in Bob's column. Let's look at the final result.

Look at Cindy's "Revision 1" (page 58). The first column starts with the year 2009. The second column shows Cindy's age – she is 32 years old. The next five columns—"Take Home Pay," "Child Support," "Spousal Support," "Retirement Withdrawal Total," and "Retirement Withdrawal Tax"—are income columns. The tax column reduces the "Total Income" column.

After finishing school, Cindy expects to earn approximately $35,000 per year. The $29,194 shown in the fourth year is her after-tax take-home pay. The 4% under "take-home pay" indicates her income is increasing at 4% per year.

The next column labeled "Child Support" indicates that she will receive $450 per month per child (or $10,800 per year) in child support for ten years until the nine-year-old child turns age 19, and then child support will decrease to $5,400 per year until the five-year-old child turns age 19. This is based on Bob's offer.

The next column is labeled "Spousal Support." Bob offered $2,000 per month ($24,000 per year) for one year and then $1,500 per month ($18,000 per year) for two additional years.

The next two columns are the "Retirement Withdrawal Total" and "Retirement Withdrawal Tax." When there is a cash flow shortage and there is no working capital, a distribution is taken out of the retirement accounts to cover the shortage. Even though there is a shortage in the first year, there is no distribution because there is enough money in the working capital accounts. Beginning in the second year the working capital is used up and a distribution is required. The tax column shows the amount of tax paid on the distribution. The distribution amount is the amount of the cash flow shortage plus the tax on the distribution. Notice the "Retirement Accounts" column is reduced by the distribution after the growth is added to the "Retirement Accounts" column.

The "Living Expenses" column represents her expenses, $51,742, minus the credit card payments of $3,865, minus the principal and interest portion of the mortgage payment, $13,589, for a net of $34,288. Her expenses decline in year 4 because her school expenses stop.

The reason the living expenses and mortgage payments are separated into separate columns is that the "Mortgage Payment" column represents the principal and interest (P&I) payment only. It is not affected by inflation. The taxes and insurance part (T&I) of the house payment are reflected in the "Living Expense" column. If the P&I were included in the "Living Expense" column, that number—affected by inflation—would eventually become skewed. The same reasoning applies to all other fixed expenses, including the credit card payments, which are shown in the "Liability Expense" column.

Notice that Cindy's living expenses have been reduced when Cindy turns ages 42 and 46—the years her children turn age 19 and leave home. Assume that Cindy no longer has the expenses associated with that child; therefore, her living expenses are reduced by the amount of child support, or $5,400.

The column labeled "Tax Liability" shows the taxes that she owes on her spousal support income. The next column is the yearly principal and interest "Mortgage Payment."

Her "Total Expenses" are $54,142. This amount is higher than the expenses that Cindy listed previously of $51,742. This is because the tax liability on the spousal support is not included in the expenses that Cindy listed.

The next column is labeled "Net Cash Flow." This shows whether there is positive or negative cash flow after netting the income columns with the expense columns. We see that Cindy has a negative $19,342 in the first year; in other words, her expenses exceed her income by $19,342.

The number from the "Net Cash Flow" column is automatically subtracted from (or added to if it is a positive number) the next column "Working Capital." It is shown earning an average of 5.5% after tax. Notice that Cindy's "Working Capital" column started out with $33,700, which is the net proceeds from the sale of the rental house. This asset is wiped out by the second year to help cover her negative cash flow.

The next column is labeled "Retirement Accounts." The assumption is that they will earn 7.5% before tax. When the "Working Capital" column is depleted, the "Retirement Account" column will automatically cover the negative cash flow less taxes and penalties if Cindy is under the age of 59 ½. After the age of 59 ½, there are no penalties; only taxes are taken out. Notice that her cash flow shortage depletes her "Retirement Account" column in the third year.

By age 34, Cindy's liquid assets have been depleted. She does have the house, but she cannot use the house to buy groceries.

The next column, "Fair Market Value Real Estate," shows the value of Cindy's house. We assumed that the value of her house will increase by 4% per year.

The "Mortgage Balance" column shows the $130,000 mortgage on Cindy's house, which has 15 years remaining at 6.5% interest. The final column, "Net Worth," is a combination of "Working Capital," "Retirement Accounts," and "FMV Real Estate," less the "Mortgage Balance" and "Liability Balance."

How does Scenario 1 affect Bob?

Let's look at Bob's "Revision 1" (page 59) to see how this scenario affects him financially.

Bob's "Take-Home Pay" column is $57,570 and is increasing at 4% per year, the same as Cindy's.

His "Living Expenses" column shows that his total annual living expenses are $24,600.

The "Child Support Expense" and "Spousal Support Expense" columns show what he pays in support.

The "Tax Liability" column shows the tax savings Bob gets by deducting the spousal support on his tax return.

His "Total Expenses" are $53,400.

The "Net Cash Flow" column shows a positive $4,170 in the first year, which is added to the "Working Capital" column and is shown earning an average of 5.5% per year after tax.

We placed his business in the "Business" column, which shows the value of his business increasing at 4% per year.

Bob's "Net Worth" column is the sum of all his assets minus his liabilities.

The graph of Bob and Cindy's net worth based on the previous assumptions (page 56) indicates that the future does not appear to be financially equitable.

Scenario 2

What changes can be made in Scenario 1 to make this a more equitable settlement? The following changes represent Scenario 2.

- Bob will assume the debt of $22,600. Note that his expenses increase in Scenario 2 to include the debt payments, and Cindy's expenses decrease.

- A property settlement note of $18,350 is paid to Cindy. The payments are $4,155 per year for five years (assuming 5% interest). This is shown in the "Settlement Note" column. Now there is an equal split of the assets. These payments help Cindy when she is earning no income.

- Bob will pay Cindy spousal support of $24,000 for three years.

The credit card payments and the liability balance are no longer on Cindy's spreadsheet. She is receiving payments from the settlement note, which are shown on the spreadsheet. In addition, her spousal support stays at $24,000 for the first three years while she is not working.

Notice that Scenario 2 helps Cindy a bit but obviously not enough. She continues to have negative cash flow for the first fifteen years. The problem is that she is too emotionally tied to the house which she cannot afford. Her house payments of $1,500 per month (PITI), combined with no earned income for three years, create a financial disaster for her.

How does Scenario 2 affect Bob?

Look at Bob's "Revision 2" (page 63). Bob is now paying the credit card debt, and he is also making payments for the property settlement note. The property settlement note is shown in two places: the "Settlement Expense" column and as a debt in the "Note Balance" column.

The debt payments, the settlement note payments, and the increased spousal support have all contributed to Bob having negative cash flow in the first three years.

Scenario 3

Let's see what happens if Cindy sells the house and moves into the rental. The property settlement note will change because the cash proceeds from the sale of the house are less than the value of the house, due to the expenses for the sale. The value of the rental also goes up because there are no selling expenses for it. Bob will also pay spousal support of $24,000 per year for the first three years and then it declines to $12,000 for the next three years.

Notice that Cindy's "Take Home Pay" is still the same; she is still going to school for three years before bringing home $29,194 per year.

The "Child Support" is the same.

The "Spousal Support" column shows income of $24,000 per year for the first three years and $12,000 for the next three years.

The "Settlement Note" column shows that the payments have gone up. The settlement note has increased to $22,900 because the home is sold prior to the divorce and Cindy gets the proceeds from the sale less the selling expenses and mortgage balance.

In Scenario 3, Cindy's mortgage payment is much lower. In some cases, the living expenses also decline because the property taxes, utilities, and repairs would probably be lower than in the bigger marital home. She no longer has the $3,865 per year for credit card payments. The "Tax Liability" on her spousal support has changed to reflect the different amount.

This is a big financial change for Cindy. She no longer has negative cash flow, except for a minor amount in year three.

When the house is sold and the selling costs and the mortgage balance are deducted from the proceeds, the remaining balance is added to the "Working Capital."

Look at the "FMV Real Estate" column. Notice that the value of her house is now $90,000 and the "Mortgage Balance" is $50,000. This shows that she is now living in the rental house.

The "Mortgage Payments" column shows the reduction in the monthly payment.

Cindy now has the proceeds from selling the house to add to her "Working Capital" column. The proceeds have increased from $33,700 for the rental to $74,600 for the house. The proceeds will last much longer if she is careful with her spending.

How does Scenario 3 affect Bob?

The higher spousal support gives him negative cash flow for the first three years. It will be very tight for him in those first three years.

As you can see, it doesn't make economic sense for Cindy to keep a house with a payment of $1,500 per month when she has no income and she is relying on spousal support to make that payment for her. Another option for someone who does not have a second home is to rent. This is a case that will take a lot of counseling on cash flow and budgeting. Both parties must understand that whatever scenario is followed, it will have a major impact on their relationship and parenting skills and financial and emotional wellbeing.

Bob's Proposal – Scenario 1

Bob and Cindy's Asset List

Item	Value	Cindy	Bob
Home			
FMV	220,000		
Mortgage	130,000		
Equity	90,000	90,000	
Rental Property			
FMV	90,000		
Mortgage	50,000		
Selling costs	(6,300)		
Equity	33,700	33,700	
Business	200,000		200,000
IRAs	17,000	17,000	
Debt	(22,600)	(22,600)	
TOTAL	**$318,100**	**$118,100**	**$200,000**

Bob and Cindy Case Study – Revisions 1, 2, and 3 start on page 56.

Bob and Cindy   Revision: 1

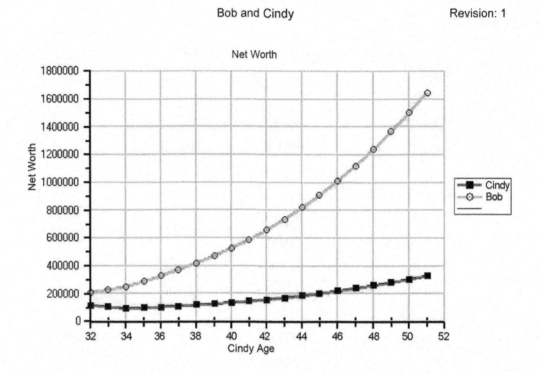

Net Worth

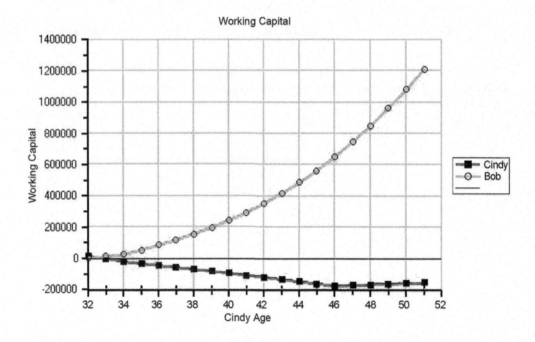

Working Capital

Bob and Cindy Jones   Revision: 1

Asset Breakdown

	Source	Value Date	Cindy	Bob	Total
Matrimonial Home			90,000	0	90,000
Business	Bob's Business		0	200,000	200,000
Cash	Sale of Rental Property		33,700	0	33,700
IRA			17,000	0	17,000
Installment Loan			(22,600)	0	(22,600)
			$118,100	**$200,000**	**$318,100**

Cindy Jones   Bob and Cindy Jones   Revision: 1

Year	Age	Take Home Pay 4.00%	Child Support 0.00%	Spousal Support 0.00%	Retirement Withdrawal Total	Retirement Withdrawal Tax	Total Income	Living Expenses 4.00%	Liability Expense	Tax Liability	Mortgage Payment	Total Expenses	Net Cash Flow	Working Capital 5.50%	Retirement Accounts 7.50%	FMV Real Estate	Mortgage Balance	Liability Balance	Net Worth
2009	32		10,800	24,000			34,800	34,288	3,865	2,400	13,589	54,142	(19,342)	33,700	17,000	220,000	(130,000)	(22,600)	118,100
2010	33		10,800	18,000	11,263	2,253	37,810	35,660	3,865	1,800	13,589	54,913	(17,103)	16,212	18,275	228,800	(124,705)	(22,180)	116,402
2011	34		10,800	18,000	9,012	1,802	36,009	37,086	3,865	1,800	13,589	56,340	(20,331)		8,363	237,952	(119,055)	(21,631)	105,589
2012	35	29,194	10,800				39,994	34,369	3,865		13,589	51,823	(11,829)	(20,331)		247,470	(113,027)	(21,121)	92,991
2013	36	30,362	10,800				41,162	35,744	3,865		13,589	53,198	(12,036)	(32,160)		257,369	(106,595)	(20,458)	98,156
2014	37	31,576	10,800				42,376	37,174	3,865		13,589	54,628	(12,252)	(44,196)		267,664	(99,732)	(19,694)	104,051
2015	38	32,839	10,800				43,639	38,661	3,865		13,589	56,115	(12,475)	(56,448)		278,370	(92,410)	(18,784)	110,729
2016	39	34,153	10,800				44,953	40,207	3,865		13,589	57,661	(12,708)	(68,923)		289,505	(84,597)	(17,734)	118,250
2017	40	35,519	10,800				46,319	41,816	3,865		13,589	59,269	(12,951)	(81,631)		301,085	(76,261)	(16,511)	126,681
2018	41	36,940	10,800				47,740	43,488	3,865		13,589	60,942	(13,202)	(94,562)		313,129	(67,367)	(15,087)	136,092
2019	42	38,417	5,400				43,817	39,828	3,865		13,589	57,282	(13,464)	(107,784)		325,654	(57,877)	(13,428)	146,564
2020	43	39,954	5,400				45,354	41,421	3,865		13,589	58,875	(13,521)	(121,249)		338,680	(47,752)	(11,494)	158,185
2021	44	41,552	5,400				46,952	43,078	3,865		13,589	60,532	(13,579)	(134,769)		352,227	(36,949)	(9,242)	171,267
2022	45	43,214	5,400				48,614	44,801	3,865		13,589	62,255	(13,640)	(148,349)		366,316	(25,422)	(6,618)	185,928
2023	46	44,943					44,943	41,193	3,865		13,589	58,647	(13,704)	(161,989)		380,969	(13,123)	(3,561)	202,296
2024	47	46,741					46,741	42,840				42,840	3,900	(175,693)		396,208			220,515
2025	48	48,610					48,610	44,554				44,554	4,056	(171,793)		412,056			240,263
2026	49	50,555					50,555	46,336				46,336	4,218	(167,737)		428,538			260,801
2027	50	52,577					52,577	48,190				48,190	4,387	(163,519)		445,680			282,161
2028	51	54,680					54,680	50,117				50,117	4,563	(159,132)		463,507			304,375

Bob Jones   Bob and Cindy Jones   Revision: 1

Year	Age	Take Home Pay 4.00%	Total Income	Living Expenses 4.00%	Child S. Expense 0.00%	Spousal S Expense 0.00%	Tax Liability	Total Expenses	Net Cash Flow	Working Capital 5.50%	Business 4.00%	Net Worth
2009	33	57,570	57,570	24,600	10,800	24,000	(6,000)	53,400	4,170	4,170	200,000	200,000
2010	34	59,873	59,873	25,584	10,800	18,000	(4,500)	49,884	9,989	14,388	208,000	212,170
2011	35	62,268	62,268	26,607	10,800	18,000	(4,500)	50,907	11,360	26,540	216,320	230,708
2012	36	64,758	64,758	27,672	10,800			38,472	26,287	54,286	224,973	251,513
2013	37	67,349	67,349	28,779	10,800			39,579	27,770	85,042	233,972	288,258
2014	38	70,043	70,043	29,930	10,800			40,730	29,313	119,033	243,331	328,373
2015	39	72,844	72,844	31,127	10,800			41,927	30,918	156,497	253,064	372,096
2016	40	75,758	75,758	32,372	10,800			43,172	32,586	197,691	263,186	419,683
2017	41	78,789	78,789	33,667	10,800			44,467	34,322	242,885	273,714	471,404
2018	42	81,940	81,940	35,013	10,800			45,813	36,127	292,371	284,662	527,548
2019	43	85,218	85,218	36,414	5,400			41,814	43,404	351,855	296,049	588,419
2020	44	88,626	88,626	37,871	5,400			43,271	45,356	416,562	307,891	659,745
2021	45	92,171	92,171	39,385	5,400			44,785	47,386	486,859	320,206	736,769
2022	46	95,858	95,858	40,961	5,400			46,361	49,497	563,134	333,015	819,874
2023	47	99,693	99,693	42,599				42,599	57,093	651,200	346,335	909,469
2024	48	103,680	103,680	44,303				44,303	59,377	746,393	360,189	1,011,389
2025	49	107,828	107,828	46,075				46,075	61,752	849,197	374,596	1,120,989
2026	50	112,141	112,141	47,918				47,918	64,222	960,125	389,580	1,238,777
2027	51	116,626	116,626	49,835				49,835	66,791	1,079,723	405,163	1,365,288
2028	52	121,291	121,291	51,828				51,828	69,463	1,208,571	421,370	1,501,093
											438,225	1,646,795

Bob and Cindy   Revision: 2

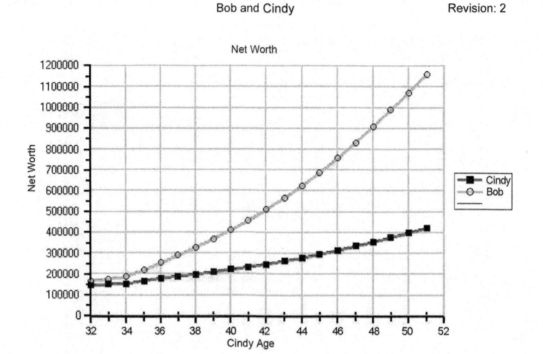

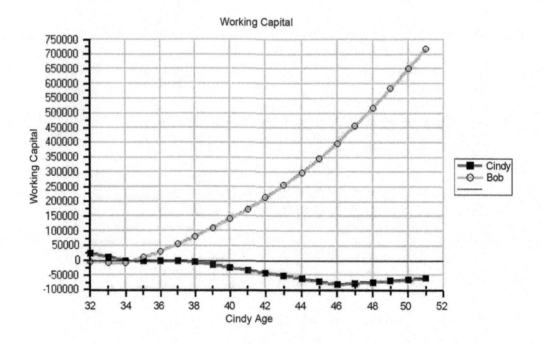

Bob and Cindy Jones   Revision: 2

Asset Breakdown

	Source	Value Date	Cindy	Bob	Total
Matrimonial Home			90,000	0	90,000
Business	Bob's Business		0	200,000	200,000
Cash	Sale of Rental Property Net Proceeds Less costs		33,700	0	33,700
IRA			17,000	0	17,000
Installment Loan			0	(22,600)	(22,600)
Settlement Note			18,350	(18,350)	0
			$159,050	**$159,050**	**$318,100**

Cindy Jones   Bob and Cindy Jones   Revision: 2

Year	Age	Take Home Pay 4.00%	Child Support 0.00%	Spousal Support 0.00%	Settlement Note	Retirement Withdrawal Total	Retirement Withdrawal Tax	Total Income	Living Expenses 4.00%	Tax Liability	Mortgage Payment	Total Expenses	Net Cash Flow	Working Capital 5.50%	Retirement Accounts 7.50%	FMV Real Estate	Mortgage Balance	Net Worth
2009	32		10,800	24,000	4,155			38,955	34,288	2,400	13,589	50,277	(11,322)	33,700	17,000	220,000	(130,000)	140,700
2010	33		10,800	24,000	4,155			38,955	35,660	2,400	13,589	51,649	(12,693)	24,232	18,275	228,800	(124,705)	146,602
2011	34		10,800	24,000	4,155	676	135	39,496	37,086	2,400	13,589	53,075	(13,579)	12,871	19,646	237,952	(119,055)	151,414
2012	35	29,194	10,800		4,155	4,761	952	47,959	34,363		13,589	47,952			20,443	247,470	(113,027)	154,886
2013	36	30,362	10,800		4,155	5,020	1,004	49,333	35,744		13,589	49,333			17,215	257,369	(106,595)	167,989
2014	37	31,576	10,800			10,484	2,097	50,763	37,174		13,589	50,763			13,486	267,664	(99,732)	181,417
2015	38	32,839	10,800			4,315	863	47,091	38,661		13,589	52,250	(5,159)		4,014	278,370	(92,410)	189,974
2016	39	34,153	10,800					44,953	40,207		13,589	53,797	(8,844)	(5,159)		289,505	(84,597)	199,748
2017	40	35,519	10,800					46,319	41,816		13,589	55,405	(9,086)	(14,003)		301,085	(76,261)	210,821
2018	41	36,940	10,800					47,740	43,488		13,589	57,077	(9,338)	(23,089)		313,129	(67,367)	222,673
2019	42	38,417	5,400					43,817	39,828		13,589	53,417	(9,600)	(32,426)		325,654	(57,877)	235,350
2020	43	39,954	5,400					45,354	41,421		13,589	55,010	(9,656)	(42,026)		338,680	(47,752)	248,902
2021	44	41,552	5,400					46,952	43,078		13,589	56,667	(9,715)	(51,682)		352,227	(36,949)	263,596
2022	45	43,214	5,400					48,614	44,801		13,589	58,390	(9,776)	(61,397)		366,316	(25,422)	279,498
2023	46	44,943						44,943	41,193		13,589	54,782	(9,839)	(71,173)		380,969	(13,123)	296,673
2024	47	46,741						46,741	42,840			42,840	3,900	(81,012)		396,208		315,196
2025	48	48,610						48,610	44,554			44,554	4,056	(77,112)		412,056		334,944
2026	49	50,555						50,555	46,336			46,336	4,218	(73,056)		428,538		355,482
2027	50	52,577						52,577	48,190			48,190	4,387	(68,838)		445,680		376,842
2028	51	54,680						54,680	50,117			50,117	4,563	(64,451)		463,507		399,056
														(59,888)		482,047		422,159

Bob Jones   Bob and Cindy Jones   Revision: 2

Year	Age	Take Home Pay 4.00%	Total Income	Living Expenses 4.00%	Child S. Expense 0.00%	Spousal S Expense 0.00%	Liability Expense	Tax Liability	Settlement Expense	Total Expenses	Net Cash Flow	Working Capital 5.50%	Business 4.00%	Note Balance	Liability Balance	Net Worth
2009	33	57,570	57,570	24,600	10,800	24,000	3,865	(6,000)	4,155	61,420	(3,850)	(3,850)	200,000	(18,350)	(22,600)	159,050
2010	34	59,873	59,873	25,584	10,800	24,000	3,865	(6,000)	4,155	62,404	(2,531)	(6,381)	208,000	(15,037)	(22,180)	166,933
2011	35	62,268	62,268	26,607	10,800	24,000	3,865	(6,000)	4,155	63,427	(1,160)	(7,541)	216,320	(11,554)	(21,691)	176,693
2012	36	64,758	64,758	27,672	10,800		3,865		4,155	46,492	18,267	10,726	224,973	(7,893)	(21,121)	188,417
2013	37	67,349	67,349	28,779	10,800		3,865		4,155	47,599	19,750	30,476	233,972	(4,045)	(20,458)	220,195
2014	38	70,043	70,043	29,930	10,800		3,865			44,594	25,448	55,924	243,331		(19,684)	254,122
2015	39	72,844	72,844	31,127	10,800		3,865			45,791	27,053	82,977	253,064		(18,784)	290,204
2016	40	75,758	75,758	32,372	10,800		3,865			47,037	28,722	111,699	263,186		(17,734)	328,429
2017	41	78,789	78,789	33,667	10,800		3,865			48,331	30,457	142,156	273,714		(16,511)	368,901
2018	42	81,940	81,940	35,013	10,800		3,865			49,678	32,262	174,418	284,662		(15,087)	411,731
2019	43	85,218	85,218	36,414	5,400		3,865			45,679	39,539	213,957	296,049		(13,428)	457,039
2020	44	88,626	88,626	37,871	5,400		3,865			47,135	41,491	255,448	307,891		(11,494)	510,353
2021	45	92,171	92,171	39,385	5,400		3,865			48,650	43,521	298,969	320,206		(9,242)	566,412
2022	46	95,858	95,858	40,961	5,400		3,865			50,225	45,633	344,602	333,015		(6,618)	625,366
2023	47	99,693	99,693	42,599			3,865			46,464	53,229	397,831	346,335		(3,561)	687,376
2024	48	103,680	103,680	44,303						44,303	59,377	457,208	360,189			758,020
2025	49	107,828	107,828	46,075						46,075	61,752	518,960	374,596			831,804
2026	50	112,141	112,141	47,918						47,918	64,222	583,182	389,580			908,540
2027	51	116,626	116,626	49,835						49,835	66,791	649,974	405,163			988,346
2028	52	121,291	121,291	51,828						51,828	69,463	719,436	421,370			1,071,343
													438,225			1,157,661

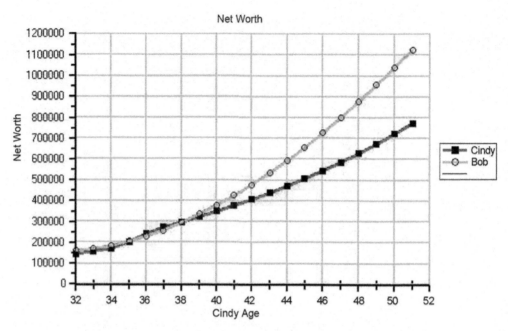

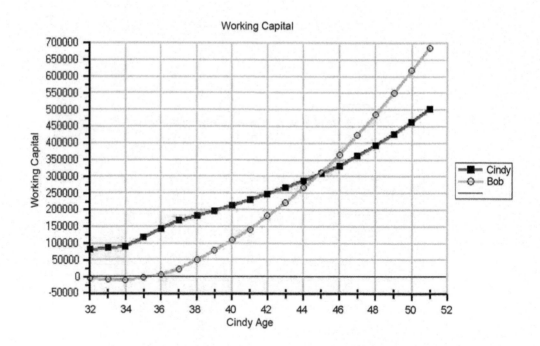

Bob and Cindy Jones   Revision: 3

Asset Breakdown

	Source	Value Date	Cindy	Bob	Total
Matrimonial Home			40,000	0	40,000
Business	Bob's Business		0	200,000	200,000
Cash	Sale of Marital Home Net Proceeds Less costs		74,600	0	74,600
IRA			17,000	0	17,000
Installment Loan			0	(22,600)	(22,600)
Settlement Note			22,900	(22,900)	0
			$154,500	**$154,500**	**$309,000**

Cindy Jones   Bob and Cindy Jones   Revision: 3

Year	Age	Take Home Pay 4.00%	Child Support 0.00%	Spousal Support 0.00%	Settlement Note	Total Income	Living Expenses 4.00%	Tax Liability	Mortgage Payment	Total Expenses	Net Cash Flow	Working Capital 5.50%	Retirement Accounts 7.50%	FMV Real Estate	Mortgage Balance	Net Worth
												74,600	17,000	90,000	(50,000)	131,600
2009	32		10,800	24,000	5,186	39,986	30,050	2,400	5,227	37,677	2,309	81,012	18,275	93,600	(47,963)	144,924
2010	33		10,800	24,000	5,186	39,986	31,252	2,400	5,227	38,879	1,107	86,575	19,646	97,344	(45,790)	157,774
2011	34		10,800	24,000	5,186	39,986	32,502	2,400	5,227	40,129	(143)	91,194	21,119	101,238	(43,472)	170,079
2012	35	29,194	10,800	12,000	5,186	57,180	29,602	1,200	5,227	36,029	21,151	117,360	22,703	105,287	(40,998)	204,353
2013	36	30,362	10,800	12,000	5,186	58,348	30,786	1,200	5,227	37,213	21,135	144,950	24,406	109,499	(38,359)	240,496
2014	37	31,576	10,800	12,000		54,376	32,018	1,200	5,227	38,444	15,932	168,854	26,236	113,879	(35,542)	273,427
2015	38	32,839	10,800			43,639	33,298		5,227	38,525	5,114	183,255	28,204	118,434	(32,537)	297,355
2016	39	34,153	10,800			44,953	34,630		5,227	39,857	5,096	198,430	30,319	123,171	(29,331)	322,589
2017	40	35,519	10,800			46,319	36,016		5,227	41,242	5,077	214,421	32,593	128,098	(25,911)	349,201
2018	41	36,940	10,800			47,740	37,456		5,227	42,683	5,057	231,271	35,038	133,222	(22,261)	377,270
2019	42	38,417	5,400			43,817	33,554		5,227	38,781	5,036	249,027	37,665	138,551	(18,366)	406,877
2020	43	39,954	5,400			45,354	34,897		5,227	40,123	5,231	267,954	40,490	144,093	(14,211)	438,326
2021	44	41,552	5,400			46,952	36,292		5,227	41,519	5,433	288,124	43,527	149,857	(9,778)	471,731
2022	45	43,214	5,400			48,614	37,744		5,227	42,971	5,643	309,615	46,792	155,851	(5,047)	507,210
2023	46	44,943				44,943	33,854		5,227	39,081	5,862	332,506	50,301	162,085		544,892
2024	47	46,741				46,741	35,208			35,208	11,532	362,326	54,073	168,568		584,968
2025	48	48,610				48,610	36,616			36,616	11,994	394,248	58,129	175,311		627,688
2026	49	50,555				50,555	38,081			38,081	12,473	428,405	62,489	182,323		673,217
2027	50	52,577				52,577	39,604			39,604	12,972	464,940	67,175	189,616		721,731
2028	51	54,680				54,680	41,188			41,188	13,491	504,003	72,213	197,201		773,417

Bob Jones   Bob and Cindy Jones   Revision: 3

Year	Age	Take Home Pay 4.00%	Total Income	Living Expenses 4.00%	Child S. Expense 0.00%	Spousal S Expense 0.00%	Liability Expense	Tax Liability	Settlement Expense	Total Expenses	Net Cash Flow	Working Capital 5.50%	Business 4.00%	Note Balance	Liability Balance	Net Worth
2009	33	57,570	57,570	24,600	10,800	24,000	3,865	(6,000)	5,186	62,450	(4,880)	(4,880)	200,000	(22,900)	(22,600)	154,500
2010	34	59,873	59,873	25,584	10,800	24,000	3,865	(6,000)	5,186	63,434	(3,562)	(8,442)	208,000	(18,765)	(22,180)	162,174
2011	35	62,268	62,268	26,607	10,800	24,000	3,865	(6,000)	5,186	64,458	(2,190)	(10,632)	216,320	(14,419)	(21,691)	171,768
2012	36	64,758	64,758	27,672	10,800	12,000	3,865	(3,000)	5,186	56,522	8,236	(2,396)	224,973	(9,850)	(21,121)	183,369
2013	37	67,349	67,349	28,779	10,800	12,000	3,865	(3,000)	5,186	57,629	9,720	7,324	233,972	(5,048)	(20,458)	206,070
2014	38	70,043	70,043	29,930	10,800	12,000	3,865	(3,000)		53,594	16,448	23,772	243,331		(19,684)	230,970
2015	39	72,844	72,844	31,127	10,800		3,865			45,791	27,053	50,825	253,064		(18,784)	258,053
2016	40	75,758	75,758	32,372	10,800		3,865			47,037	28,722	79,547	263,186		(17,734)	296,277
2017	41	78,789	78,789	33,667	10,800		3,865			48,331	30,457	110,004	273,714		(16,511)	336,749
2018	42	81,940	81,940	35,013	10,800		3,865			49,678	32,262	142,266	284,662		(15,087)	379,579
2019	43	85,218	85,218	36,414	5,400		3,865			45,679	39,539	181,805	296,049		(13,428)	424,887
2020	44	88,626	88,626	37,871	5,400		3,865			47,135	41,491	223,296	307,891		(11,494)	478,201
2021	45	92,171	92,171	39,385	5,400		3,865			48,650	43,521	266,817	320,206		(9,242)	534,260
2022	46	95,858	95,858	40,961	5,400		3,865			50,225	45,633	312,450	333,015		(6,618)	593,214
2023	47	99,693	99,693	42,599			3,865			46,464	53,229	365,679	346,335		(3,561)	655,224
2024	48	103,680	103,680	44,303						44,303	59,377	425,056	360,189			725,868
2025	49	107,828	107,828	46,075						46,075	61,752	486,808	374,596			799,652
2026	50	112,141	112,141	47,918						47,918	64,222	551,031	389,580			876,388
2027	51	116,626	116,626	49,835						49,835	66,791	617,822	405,163			956,194
2028	52	121,291	121,291	51,828						51,828	69,463	687,285	438,225			1,125,509

CHAPTER 4
SPOUSAL SUPPORT
(ALIMONY/MAINTENANCE)

Learning Objectives

After completing this chapter, you will be able to:

1. State the criteria for receiving or paying spousal support.
2. Define rehabilitative maintenance.
3. Discuss how, when, and why spousal support can be modified.
4. Explain the tax issues of spousal support.
5. Differentiate between taxable vs. non-taxable spousal support, including front-loading of spousal support and recapture.
6. Explain how to guarantee spousal support through life insurance, disability insurance, or an annuity.

After deciding on a plan for dividing the property, spousal support should be reviewed. It is important to divide the property and then determine the amount of spousal support because the amount of property awarded will impact the need for and the amount of spousal support.

For all practical purposes, spousal support, alimony, and maintenance mean the same thing; they are used interchangeably. Simply put, spousal support is a series of payments from one spouse to the other, or to a third party on behalf of the recipient spouse. Generally speaking, spousal support is taxable income to the recipient and tax deductible by the payor.

Spousal support can be very important for the non-working spouse. In many long-term marriages (in some states "long-term" is defined as more than ten years), one of the spouses has not worked outside of the home or has stayed home with the children until they are older or left home. In both of these circumstances that spouse's ability to build a career may be limited. The couple may have decided, for example, that the wife would be responsible for running the household and caring for the children. In most cases, if she did hold a job, her income was less than her husband's—sometimes substantially lower. If a transfer or move occurred, it was for the benefit of his career. When they moved, she had to quit her job and start over.

When you are "fired" from the job of husband or wife, no one offers you an unemployment check. Is it any wonder, then, that spousal support often becomes a major battleground in divorce?

Deciding whether a spouse should receive spousal support (and, if so, how much) is based on different criteria depending on state law. In some states, the spouse may be awarded rehabilitative maintenance, or the payments may be modifiable or non-modifiable. Of course, as with any source of income, there are tax laws to be aware of, including laws regarding front-loading of spousal support (recapture rules), treating life-insurance payments as spousal support, and child contingency rules.

CRITERIA FOR RECEIVING OR PAYING SPOUSAL SUPPORT

Courts used to award spousal support based on "fault," which may still be a factor in some states. However, spousal support is generally based on many different factors, including:

- Need

- Ability to pay

- Length of marriage

- Previous lifestyle

- Age and health of both parties

1. Need

"Does the recipient have enough money to live on?" This would include income from earning ability and earnings from the recipient's share of marital property and separate property. Spousal support may be necessary to prevent the wife (and sometimes the husband) from becoming dependent upon welfare.

When evaluating need, minor children should also be considered. Although child support is a separate issue, the mother (if she is the custodial parent) must be able to care adequately for the children. That means a roof over the child's head, food on the table, and utilities for heat, light, and water in the home.

Even though one spouse may think spousal support is necessary, the court sometimes finds otherwise. Here's an example. Sophia wanted spousal support from her husband. However, she had a trust set aside that was separate property, and in that trust was more than $1 million. The court found that she did not need spousal support because she had property that would provide income to her.

After you have established need, how do you determine the amount? That is not so easy. A case study was given to judges at a conference to review the variety of opinions. The case involved a short-term marriage between two lawyers; during the marriage, the wife developed multiple sclerosis and was in serious condition. The judges' opinions ranged from "no alimony as it was a short-term marriage" to "lifetime alimony because of her health situation" and all points in between.

If we look at the following simplistic formula, we will see that there can be many problems.

$$\frac{\text{Husband's income} - \text{expenses}}{\text{Ability to pay}} \qquad \frac{\text{Wife's expenses} - \text{income}}{\text{Need}}$$

It is easy to say that somewhere between his ability to pay and her need is the amount of spousal support to be paid, but questions arise about their true incomes and expenses. It is not as easy as it seems.

2.   Ability to pay

To determine the ability to pay, a judge considers whether the payor can afford to pay what is needed and still have enough to live on or support a lifestyle roughly equivalent to his or her previous lifestyle.

An angry wife may say, "I want $6,000 a month," which is his entire salary. The wife is acting out of anger, which is not unusual, but it is your responsibility to get her to be more reasonable and realistic.

What about the cases where the husband's commissions and bonuses dry up when it is time to get divorced? We know that divorce causes an extreme amount of stress. After the divorce is final, his income generally goes back up. In this situation, additional income may be imputed to the husband when calculating the amount of spousal support.

For instance, there was the famous Boulder, Colorado case where the high-earning husband decided to quit his job and go into the mountains to grow mushrooms. The husband claimed he no longer had the income to pay much in spousal support. The judge ruled that the husband had the income-producing capacity and therefore the husband could grow mushrooms if he wished, but he would have to figure out how to pay the spousal support that the court awarded to his wife.

3.   Length of marriage/duration of support

A two-year marriage may not qualify a spouse for permanent spousal support, but a 25-year marriage might. However, a judge will generally consider all the economic factors in the divorce and the property division.

How long should spousal support be paid? Spousal support can be of limited duration (for a certain number of years) or open-ended (continues until it is modified or terminated). A 20-year marriage, which began when the wife was 18 and ended when she was 38, may not make her eligible for long-term spousal support. But a 20-year marriage that started when the wife was 40 and ended when she was 60 may qualify her for long-term support. One rule of thumb is that spousal support may be awarded for half the number of years they were married. However, this rule of thumb can be far from the right answer depending on other factors.

Some rules to remember about duration of spousal support payments:

- Spousal support usually stops upon the death of either party.

- Spousal support usually ends upon the remarriage of the recipient.

- Spousal support continues until it is modified (unless the decree states that the amount or duration is non-modifiable).

4. Previous lifestyle

How are the spouses accustomed to living? In a 23-year marriage where the husband earns more than $500,000 per year, he probably will not, in good faith, be able to support his claim that his wife only needs $50,000 per year in spousal support. In contrast, if a couple did not earn much money, the wife should not expect to become wealthy as a result of the divorce.

5. Age and health of both parties

The age and health of both parties are other issues to consider:

- Is either spouse disabled?

- Is either spouse retired? If so, does he or she have guaranteed permanent income?

- If either spouse is 50 years old and has never worked, it will be very difficult for him or her to find employment. That spouse may need open-ended spousal support.

REHABILITATIVE MAINTENANCE

In the 1970s, courts began to recognize the need for a transition period. It was unrealistic to expect or assume that the wife (or husband when the wife was the breadwinner) could instantly earn what her husband did, if ever. With that awakening, rehabilitative maintenance was born.

If the wife, for example, needs three years of school to finish her degree or time to update old skills, she may get rehabilitative maintenance. This will give her the temporary financial help that she needs until she is able to earn an amount sufficient to support herself.

In discussing rehabilitative maintenance, it is important to be realistic. Why? Sometimes a normal three-year degree becomes impossible while caring for three kids. Realistically, five years may be more in line. Support should not be viewed as an entitlement to be stretched until every drop is taken. Rather, it is a bridge from one "career" to the next.

Finally, depending on all other factors, particularly her age and the duration of the marriage, paying spousal support just for a rehabilitative period may not be the right result.

MODIFICATION OF SPOUSAL SUPPORT

The one constant in life is change. Given that, it does not make much sense to assume that the final spousal support settlement decided in court will apply to all future scenarios. Property division is almost always final, whereas spousal support is usually modifiable. For example, one spouse may become unemployed; the other may become ill. Change can be positive, too. One of the spouses may land a job that creates lucrative stock options and incentives; one could inherit a substantial sum of money, win a lawsuit, or even win the lottery. This type of windfall could lead to a decrease in maintenance.

To allow some flexibility to accommodate these potential changes, the court where the divorce is granted often maintains "jurisdiction" over the case. This allows any order of support to be modified when a change of circumstances makes it reasonable to do so.

These changes in circumstances include increases or decreases in the income or expenses of either or both spouses, especially when such changes were outside the control of the individual. What if the ex-wife gets a roommate who pays all the expenses? The husband's attorney could use this as a fact to reduce his current spousal support payment. Some states presume that when an ex-spouse who receives spousal support moves in with and/or marries another person, he or she needs less monetary support.

After the divorce is final and an order of support is entered, either spouse can go back into court and ask for a modification, either up or down, unless the parties stipulated that it was non-modifiable spousal support. The judge may, however, deny the request for modification. Not only that, but he or she may even rule in the opposite direction. So, before going back to court to ask for a modification, the parties should examine the position and the soundness of the evidence.

Non-modifiable spousal support is not used very often because it could be very detrimental to either party, but it can also be advantageous in some cases. For example, Tom is ordered to pay Elaine non-modifiable spousal support for six years. This means that even if Elaine remarries in two years (provided that the order says the obligation survives remarriage), Tom will have to pay her four more years of spousal support. While this appears to be a great deal for Elaine, it can work against her. What if she becomes disabled or otherwise needs more income? She cannot get more. After six years, all payments stop. Legally, Elaine has no way to continue receiving the spousal support.

What happens if—after spousal support is set up—the husband decides to retire early? He will not want to pay spousal support anymore. To change the original order, he will have to go back to court and have the spousal support changed by a new court order. This means money is spent; both parties will have to hire attorneys to get the spousal support changed. Even if they both agree, they have to draw up a new agreement.

Sometimes the parties cannot settle and the case will end up in court. If the recipient does not want to reduce the spousal support, but the payor wants to completely stop paying, the recipient may be receptive to some decrease in spousal support but not a decrease to zero. If they cannot agree on the amount, they end up in front of a judge.

For the above reasons, many payors of spousal support prefer the term to be non-modifiable. They know there will be a predetermined end to the stream of payments. It is easier to accept rather than worry about the uncertainty of when everything will end. However, depending on the facts of the case and the law, the recipient may only agree to this if there is a disproportionate division of property in his or her favor.

TAX ISSUES OF SPOUSAL SUPPORT

To be considered spousal support, the payments must meet all of the following requirements:

1. All payments must be made in cash, check, or money order.

2. There must be a written court order or separation agreement.

3. The couple may not agree that the payments are not to receive spousal support tax treatment.

4. They may not be residing in the same household.

5. The payments must terminate upon the payee's death.

6. They may not file a joint tax return.

7. No portion may be considered child support.

Let's look at each requirement in more detail:

1. **In order to qualify as spousal support, payments made from one spouse to the other must be made in cash or the equivalent of cash. A transfer of property or the performance of a service does not qualify as spousal support.**

    • *It is possible for payments made to a third party on behalf of his or her spouse to qualify as spousal support.*

Under the terms of their divorce decree, Stanley is required to pay his ex-wife, Marilyn, $5,000 per year for the next five years. Six months after the decree is entered, Marilyn decides to return to school to qualify for a better paying job. She calls Stanley and asks him to pay her $2,500 tuition bill instead of sending her the monthly spousal support checks. Stanley agrees and on September 4 pays $2,500 for Marilyn's first semester tuition. For Stanley to deduct this payment as spousal support, he must obtain a written statement from Marilyn indicating that they agreed that his payment of the tuition was spousal support. This written statement must be received before Stanley files his original (not an amended) income tax return.

As tax return time approaches, Stanley is eager to get his tax refund. He files his return without waiting for the written statement from Marilyn. He may not deduct the payments as spousal support because he failed to get the required written statement before the return was filed.

Here is another example. Under the terms of their separation agreement, Robert must pay the mortgage, real estate taxes, and insurance premiums on a house owned solely by his ex-wife, Julia. Robert may deduct these payments as spousal support. Julia must include the payments in her income, but she is entitled to claim deductions for the amount of the real estate taxes and mortgage interest if she itemizes her deductions.

- If the payor pays rent on the ex-spouse's apartment, the rent may be considered spousal support. This must be in the divorce decree.

- If the payor pays the mortgage for the ex-spouse, the payment may be considered spousal support. This must be in in the agreement.

- If the payor pays the mortgage on the house owned by the payor, the payment is not considered to be spousal support.

- If the payee spouse owns the life insurance policy on the life of the payor, the payments made by the payor will qualify as spousal support if so stated in the divorce decree.

The bottom line: If the payor is making payments on something owned by the payor for the benefit of the ex-spouse, the payments do not qualify as spousal support. If the payor makes payments on something owned by the ex-spouse, the payments do qualify if it is stated in the divorce decree.

- *Payments made to maintain property owned by the payor do not qualify as spousal support.*

Assume the same facts from above, except that Robert and Julia own the residence as joint tenants. Since he has a 50% ownership interest in the house, Robert may deduct only half of the payments as spousal support. However, he is entitled to claim deductions for interest and property taxes with respect to his half of the mortgage payments and property taxes. Similarly, Julia must report half of the payments as income and can only claim half of the deductible interest and property taxes.

- *Transfer of services does not qualify as spousal support.*

    Assume that Jake offered to mow his ex-wife's lawn. He figured that would be worth $550 and he could deduct it as spousal support. Sorry Jake, it will not qualify as spousal support.

2. **There must be a written separation agreement or a court order for the payments to qualify as spousal support.**

    As an example, Craig and Sally are separated. Craig sends Sally a letter offering to pay her $400 a month in spousal support. Sally feels this is a slap in the face since she raised their kids and kept his house clean for 18 years. She does not respond. Craig starts sending her $400 per month. Sally cashes the checks. Since there is no written agreement, he may not deduct the payments as spousal support.

    Here's another example. According to their divorce decree, Allen is to send Marian $750 per month in spousal support for 10 years. Two years after their divorce, Marian loses her job and prevails on Allen's good nature to increase her spousal support for six months until she gets started in a new job. He starts sending her an extra $200 per month. This was an oral agreement, not written. No post-decree modification was made, and he may not deduct the additional amounts.

3. **The divorcing couple must not opt out of spousal support treatment for federal income tax purposes.**

    Spousal support is taxable to the person who receives it and tax deductible by the person who pays it unless they agreed in the divorce decree that the spousal support would not be deductible.

4. **The divorcing couple may not be members of the same household at the time payment is made after the final decree.**

    Sometimes a couple gets divorced but neither can afford to move. They reach an agreement: she lives upstairs and he lives downstairs. He pays her spousal support as specified in the decree, but he cannot deduct it on his tax return. Since they live in the same house, it is not considered spousal support. However, for temporary spousal support, the parties may be members of the same household.

5. **The obligation to make payments must terminate upon the recipient's death.**

    The obligation may cease upon the death of either the payor or the payee. Spousal support payments may survive the payor's death if it is stipulated in the divorce decree.

6. **The ex-spouses may not file a joint tax return.**

    Many couples incorrectly file a joint tax return in the year their divorce became final. Their filing status is determined based on their marital status as of December 31 of the year they are filing. If they are divorced during the year of 2014, on December 31, 2014, they are not married and may not file a joint return.

7. **If any portion of the payment is considered child support, then that portion cannot be treated as spousal support.**

    If spousal support is reduced six months either before or after the date when a child reaches the age of 18, 21, or the age of majority in his or her state, the amount of the reduction is considered child support and not spousal support. (See a more complete discussion in Chapter 5).

TAXABLE VS. NON-TAXABLE SPOUSAL SUPPORT

During the temporary separation period and until the divorce is final, the couple can decide whether payments to one spouse are taxable or non-taxable. Generally, any money that is paid to a spouse before a permanent order is not considered spousal support. However, some temporary orders consider the payments to be spousal support and taxable. Written agreements and good communication are essential here. Nothing should ever be assumed by either party or attorney.

Front-Loading of Spousal Support

Generally, if the payor spouse wants to deduct spousal support in excess of $15,000 without being subject to recapture, the payments must last for at least three years and they may not decrease by more than $15,000 over the first three post-separation years. The recapture rules were designed to prevent nondeductible property settlement payments from being deducted as spousal support. The rules come into effect to the extent that spousal support payments decrease annually in excess of $15,000 during the first three calendar years.

To the extent that the payor spouse has paid "excess spousal support," the excess spousal support is to be recaptured in the payor spouse's taxable income beginning in the third year post-separation IRC §71(f)(1)(A). The payee spouse is entitled to deduct the recaptured amount from gross income in the third post-separation year [IRC §71(f)(1)(B)].

For example, Trish tells her husband Robert that, after the divorce, she plans to go back to school for three years and finish her degree. Then she will be able to get a job that will pay her $30,000 a year and she will no longer need spousal support. She asks Robert if he will support her for those three years. He agrees. Her expenses for those three years, including school costs, are $60,000 the first year, $45,000 in the second year, and $30,000 the third year.

Here is what Robert's annual payments look like:

First year	$60,000
Second year	$45,000
Third year	$30,000

The problem is that if the payments drop by more than $15,000 over the first three years, then recapture is triggered on the amount over $15,000. In Robert's case, the spousal support dropped by $15,000 from Year 1 to Year 2 and then by $15,000 from Year 2 to Year 3. Robert will have to pay tax on the recaptured spousal support. He will report $7,500 of additional income on his tax return in the third post-separation year. The recapture calculations will be covered in more detail in Module 3. For now, there are many free recapture calculators on the Internet if you want to check the numbers.

The recapture rules do not apply if:

- Either spouse dies before the end of the third post-separation year or the spouse entitled to receive the payments remarries before the end of the third post-separation year [IRC §71(f)(5)(A)(i & ii)].

- The payment amount fluctuates for reasons not within the control of the payor spouse. For example, the payments may be a fixed percentage of income from a business or property or from compensation for employment [IRC §71(f)(5)(C)].

  Note: There is no exception for co-habitation. If there is a termination of spousal support clause in the decree that includes co-habitation, then it could trigger recapture.

For example, Bert agrees to pay Maggie 25% of the net income from his farm each year for a period of three years. In the first year, the net income from the farm was $120,000, and Bert sent Maggie a check for $30,000. During the second year, the area was hit by severe weather and most of his crops were wiped out. That year, the farm's net income was only $32,000, so Bert sent Maggie a check for $8,000. In the third year, the farming business suffered a loss of $10,000 and Bert did not make a payment to Maggie that year. In this case, no recapture is required because the fluctuations were not in Bert's control.

GUARANTEEING SPOUSAL SUPPORT

Even though the divorce decree stipulates one spouse is to pay the other a specified amount of spousal support over a certain period of time, that does not mean it will happen. There are several ways an ex-spouse can get out of making the payments. Fortunately, there are several ways to guard against this and to guarantee that the payments will be made. These include life insurance, disability insurance, and annuities.

Life Insurance

Spousal support payments usually stop upon the death of the payor. Therefore, it should be stipulated in the divorce decree that life insurance will be carried on the life of the payor to replace spousal support in the event of the payor's death. If a new policy is to be purchased, it should be done before the divorce is final.

For example: Alex agreed to buy a life insurance policy to insure his spousal support payments to Sarah. After the divorce was final, he applied for the insurance and took his health exam. He was found to be uninsurable. If Sarah had known this before the divorce, her attorney would have asked for a different settlement. It was now too late.

The recipient spouse should either own the life insurance or be an irrevocable beneficiary for two reasons: to ensure that the premiums are paid and to ensure the payments are taxed like spousal support.

1. **To ensure that the premiums are paid.** For example: Bernie was ordered by the court to purchase a $50,000 life insurance policy on his life payable to Betty in the event of his death. A few years later, Bernie got tired of making the insurance payments and canceled the life insurance policy. No one knew that Bernie had canceled the policy. When he died, there was no insurance to cover Betty's spousal support. If Betty had been the owner of the policy, she would have received notice that the policy was going to lapse.

2. **Tax treatment.** If the beneficiary spouse either owns the policy or is an irrevocable beneficiary and the premium payments are made under a legal obligation imposed by the divorce decree, the premiums are considered spousal support and tax deductible by the payor and taxable to the recipient.

Disability Insurance

A second way to guarantee the stream of spousal support income is to have disability insurance on the payor's ability to earn income. Assume, for example, that Sam is to pay his ex-wife Mary spousal support of $1,200 per month based on his salary of $6,000 per month. Then he becomes disabled. Since Sam has disability insurance and he receives $4,000 per month tax-free, he can continue making spousal support payments. If Sam did not have disability insurance, he would probably go back to court and ask to have the spousal support modified.

Annuity

A third way to guarantee spousal support is to have the payor buy an annuity that pays a monthly stream of income equal to the spousal support payment.

Assume that Ted buys a $200,000 annuity that will pay out $850 per month (the agreed-upon spousal support payment) in interest only. If the payment represents interest-only payments, they are taxable to him as income, but deductible by him as spousal support. His wife, Judy, will pay taxes on the payments. This way, the payment is always made on time, the payor does not need to worry about it, the recipient does not have to worry about it, and the principal can still belong to the payor. At the end of the agreed-upon term of spousal support, Ted can stop the interest-only payments.

If the agreed-upon spousal support is $1,000 per month and Ted chooses to annuitize the annuity and receive $1,000 per month, part of the payment will be taxable to him, say $850, but he will be able to deduct the whole $1,000 as spousal support payments. At the end of the term of spousal support, he will continue to receive $1,000 per month.

CHAPTER 5
CHILD SUPPORT

Learning Objectives

After completing this chapter, you will be able to:

1. State the child support guidelines.
2. Discuss how, when, and why child support can be modified.
3. List the tax exemptions for children.
4. Define the child contingency rule, including the six-month rule and the multiple reduction rule.
5. Recognize recession-related issues.

Every parent is obligated to support his or her children, regardless of the parents' marital status. In a divorce situation, the non-custodial parent is usually ordered to pay child support to the custodial parent from which the custodial parent pays the child's expenses.

The federal government passed laws cutting federal financial assistance for states that did not implement child support guidelines. As a result, all states have child support guidelines. The guidelines help the courts decide the amount of child support to be paid. You should review the guidelines in the states where you practice. You should be able to acquire software to calculate child support payments that follow your state guidelines.

The courts in each state have the power to deviate from the child support guidelines (award a different amount). The state statutes set out the acceptable deviations. The parents can also agree to a different amount provided that the court approves the agreement.

States have upper income limits for application of the child support guidelines. If the parents' income exceeds specified limits in their state, the parents are not bound by the child support guidelines.

Some child support guideline formulas are based on the ratio of each parent's income as well as the percentage of time the child spends with each parent, and takes into consideration the amount of spousal support paid to the custodial parent.

Here is an example of the application of an income ratio child support guideline formula.

Paul's gross income is $4,300 a month, and Becky's gross income is $900 a month. Together, they earn $5,200.

Paul	$4,300	83%
Becky	$900	17%
	$5,200	

Paul is earning 83% of their total income, and Becky is earning 17%. They have two children. The child support guidelines for two children dictate that the children need $983 per month. Using the guidelines, take 83% of the suggested monthly payment of $983, and you will determine that Paul owes Becky $816 in monthly child support if he pays no spousal support.

Now assume that Paul is going to pay Becky spousal support of $1,000 a month. At this point, you would subtract the $1,000 from his income and add it to Becky's income.

Paul	$4,300	–	$1,000	=	$3,300	63%
Becky	$900	+	$1,000	=	$1,900	37%
	$5,200				$5,200	

The totals stay the same but the percentages change. Now, his percentage is 63%. Using the same guideline formula, multiply $983 by 63%, and you determine that Paul will pay $620 per month instead of $816.

The rule of thumb with this type of a formula is: as spousal support increases, child support decreases. Unfortunately, the amount of child support paid is often less than the actual amount required to meet the needs of growing children.

Another problem is that many times child support is not paid at all. The husband is suspicious or angry and thinks, "I am not sure that my ex-wife will spend the money on the children…she'll probably spend it on herself!" Child support is often based on income so, obviously, it is based on some kind of lifestyle that was established during the marriage.

The husband thinks: "If I want my children to live in this kind of a house, I have to pay enough child support to cover the house payment. That means my ex-wife is going to be there, too." So, many times the husband will get angry because his ex-wife is getting spousal support on top of child support. Or, if she is not getting spousal support, he feels that she is living off the child support. However, there are many fathers who understand that for the children to live in the kind of house they are accustomed to, the ex-wife must be with the children.

Paul and Becky present a very simplistic example. There are other factors that are considered, such as whether he is paying for childcare, health insurance, and/or education or school expenses. These factors would require adjustments to the child support amount. Also, if there are four children and three will live with the mother and one with the father, there would be an impact on the financial picture. Another factor that affects the outcome is the percentage of time the children live with the non-custodial parent according to the parenting schedule.

MODIFYING CHILD SUPPORT

What happens when circumstances change after the divorce is final? Perhaps one ex-spouse loses his or her job or becomes disabled or one of them wins the lottery. Child support is always modifiable.

The courts really try to protect the children. Therefore, even though couples with young children can agree on almost any settlement issue, they cannot generally enter a binding agreement to waive the amount or duration of child support.

The property settlement is final and you usually cannot change anything about it unless you can prove fraud or other state statutory factors. However, child support and spousal support can be modified for a substantial change in circumstances, unless there was an agreement to the contrary not to change the spousal support.

How much of a change constitutes a "substantial" change in circumstances? In some states, if income changes, then the child support may be modified according to the child support guidelines.

If circumstances change, the child support generally has to be modified by the court. One spouse cannot unilaterally decide to modify the child support. Assume there are two children and child support has been set by the court. The older child decides to live with Dad during the summer. Since Dad is paying the full cost of supporting this child at his house (at least for several months), Dad says, "Now I only have to pay half the child support," and he sends a check for half the amount of child support. Because the child support was not changed by a court order, in most states Dad still owes the full amount of child support and his ex-wife could force him to pay the other half.

Or, suppose that both kids go to live with Dad during the summer. Dad says, "I do not have to pay any child support during the summer since both kids are living with me," but the court order says that he must pay every month. It does not say "nine months out of the year." Unless it is in the court order, he is liable for those payments, and his ex-wife could sue him for the child support. It is important to have written agreements as circumstances change.

INCOME TAX CONSIDERATIONS

Child support payments cannot be deducted by the payor and are not included in the income of the recipient.

If a divorced couple has only one child, that child can be claimed as an exemption by only one parent in a given year. Unless otherwise specified, the parent that has physical custody of the child for the greater portion of the calendar year generally claims the exemption.

The exemption can be traded back and forth, year to year, between the parents with a written waiver or IRS Form 8332. Once the custodial parent has executed the waiver, the non-custodial parent must attach the form to his or her income tax return. If the waiver is for more than one year, a copy of the form must be attached to the non-custodial parent's return each year.

If the divorced couple has more than one child, the parents may divide the exemptions. The children's Social Security numbers must be listed on each parent's tax return. IMPORTANT: If both parents claim the same child or children on their tax return, they are inviting an IRS audit.

For either parent to claim the exemption, the child must be in the custody of at least one parent for more than half of the calendar year. If the child lives with a grandparent or someone other than a parent for more than half of the calendar year, neither parent can claim the exemption.

CHILD CONTINGENCY RULE

If any amount of spousal support specified in the divorce decree is reduced:

a)   upon the happening of any contingency related to the child; or

b)   at a time that can be clearly associated with a contingency related to the child, then the amount of the reduction will be treated as child support, rather than spousal support. These payments will be considered child support when the payments begin [IRC §71(c)(2). Reg. § 1.71-1T(c) (Q&A) 18].

In order to prevent re-characterization of the payments, it is necessary to avoid a reduction of spousal support at a time associated with the occurrence of a child-related contingency. Sidestepping this trap is made easier by the fact that there are only two situations in which payments that would otherwise qualify as spousal support are presumed to be reduced at a time clearly associated with the occurrence of a child-related contingency.

1. Six-month rule

The first situation occurs when the spousal support payments are reduced not more than six months before or after the date on which the child reaches age 18, 21, or the age of majority in their state.

Example: Michael is to pay Susan $2,000 per month in spousal support. The amount of spousal support is to be reduced to $1,000 beginning with the January 2013 payment. Their child, Todd, was born April 5, 1995, and he will reach the age of majority (18) on April 5, 2013. The date six months before April 5, 2013 is October 5, 2012, and the date six months after is October 5, 2013. Thus, if there is any reduction in payments during the period from October 5, 2012 through October 5, 2013, it is presumed that the amount of the reduction constitutes child support and not spousal support.

- April 5, 2013: Todd's 18th birthday

- October 5, 2012 to October 5, 2013: six months before and six months after Todd's 18th birthday

- January 1, 2013: spousal support reduced from $2,000 to $1,000/month. This date falls within the October 5, 2012 to October 5, 2013 time period.

Thus, only $1,000 per month will qualify as spousal support because the reduction in the payment falls within a six-month period associated with the occurrence of a child-related contingency: Todd turning age 18.

2. Multiple reduction rule

The second situation is when there is more than one child. In this instance, if the spousal support payments are to be reduced on two or more occasions, which occur not more than one year before or after each child reaches a certain age, then it is presumed that the amount of the reduction is child support. The age at which the reduction occurs must be between 18 and 24, inclusive, and must be the same for each of the children.

Example: Ralph is to pay Theresa $2,000 per month in spousal support. Theresa has custody of their two children, Heidi and Thor. The payments are to be reduced to $1,500 per month on January 1, 2012 when Heidi is 20 years, 5 months. On January 1, 2016, the payments will be reduced to $1,000 per month when Thor is 22 years, 3 months. Each reduction in the payment will occur not more than one year before or after a different child attains the age of 21 years and 4 months. Therefore, the reductions are associated with a contingency related to the children, and are presumed to be child support.

Since both reductions occurred not more than one year before or after Heidi and Thor reached the age of 21 years and 4 months, it is presumed that $1,000 of the spousal support is actually child support.

Discussion

An attorney might think, "Johnnie is graduating from high school in five years, so let's give Mom spousal support for five years." Or he or she might say, "Since Johnnie is graduating in five years, let's give Mom spousal support of $2,000 a month for five years and then reduce it to $1,500 a month for an extra three years."

This could create a serious tax problem for Dad. If the IRS considers the reduction of $500 a month to be child support, they will make it retroactive from the beginning for a five-year period. Dad would have to amend the prior years' tax returns and pay the tax for those years. The tax consequence would be 12 x $500 = $6,000 of additional income for each tax year. However, it would all be past due, so penalties and interest might be imposed in addition to the tax that would be due. Unfortunately for Mom, the statute of limitations would preclude her from amending all five years; she can only go back three years from the date of filing. So she would only be able to amend three or possibly four years of tax returns to get a refund.

RECESSION-RELATED ISSUES

Since 2008, courts have seen a surge in the number of divorced parents coming back to request that their child support be modified due to a change in their circumstance, such as being laid off from work or losing their homes to foreclosure. Payors are asking that the amount be reduced, and recipients that the amount remain the same or be increased.

Having the child support reduced or even eliminated can have a devastating effect on the family. Some custodial parents depend on that child support to feed and clothe the children; if the payments are reduced or cease, it puts a burden on the custodial parent, who has to come up with funds another way. Some families have been forced to apply for welfare for the first time, and others have become increasingly dependent on food stamps or even risk eviction when they cannot pay the rent.

Child support payments take precedence over spousal support, so if the child support is being reduced or eliminated, it is safe to assume the same is happening to spousal support.

CHAPTER 6
SOCIAL SECURITY

Learning Objectives

After completing this chapter, you will be able to:

1. Discuss how an ex-spouse can qualify for Social Security retirement benefits based on the earnings of the ex-spouse.
2. Explain how an ex-spouse can qualify for widow's benefits.
3. Recognize divorce-related Social Security issues, including discovery requests, benefits and asset division, use of alimony to equalize benefits, and child support and benefits.

For simplicity, we will assume that the wife is the lower wage-earning spouse in the examples in this chapter. In real life, obviously, the husband could be the lower wage-earning spouse.

If a couple has been married for ten years (measured from the date of the marriage to the date that the divorce is final) or longer and they get a divorce, the wife is entitled to half of her ex-husband's Social Security retirement benefits if:

1. He is eligible to receive Social Security benefits.

2. She is not married; if she is married, she can get benefits based on her own earnings or on her current husband's earnings.

3. She is age 62 or over.

4. She is not eligible for Social Security retirement benefits based on her own earnings, which equal or exceed one-half of her ex-husband's benefits.

The husband's Social Security retirement benefits are not reduced by the amount that his ex-wife receives at retirement.

An ex-wife who is age 62 or over and has been divorced for at least two years will be able to receive benefits based on the earnings of her ex-husband regardless of whether her ex-husband has retired or applied for benefits.

If the ex-wife of a retired or disabled worker is caring for the worker's under-age-16 or disabled child, the monthly benefit equals half of the worker's benefit regardless of her age. If the ex-wife is not caring for a child, monthly benefits equal half of the ex-husband's—unless she chooses to start receiving benefits at age 62, in which case the benefit that she would receive at age 65 is reduced by approximately 25%. If the ex-wife chooses to receive the reduced benefit at age 62, she is not entitled to the full benefit upon reaching age 65. If the worker chooses to take benefits at age 62, his reduction would only be approximately 20%.

Assume that Ken will receive $750 a month in Social Security when he retires. He was married to his ex-wife, Helen, for ten years; she will be entitled to Social Security benefits of $375 (half of Ken's benefit) at age 65:

> Ken $750
> Helen $375

What if Ken gets remarried? If Ken is married to his second wife, Marci, for ten years and they get a divorce, Marci will get $375, Helen will also get $375, and Ken will still get $750. There is no limit on the number of wives who can collect. As long as Ken is married to each one for ten years or longer, they each get half of his Social Security benefit.

> Ken $750
> Helen $375
> Marci $375

What happens when Ken dies? Each wife that qualifies gets 100% of Ken's benefits. So Helen and Marci will each receive $750.

What if Helen gets remarried? If she is married at retirement time, she looks to her current husband, George, for her benefits. But if she has been married to George for ten years and they get divorced, she is entitled to half of Ken's benefits or half of George's benefits. She has a choice.

> Ken $750   George $600
> Helen's half $375   Helen's half $300

Since George is only entitled to $600 at retirement, Helen will obviously choose the higher benefits based on Ken's earnings.

Assume Helen begins working after the kids are adults and that by the time she retires, she will earn $450 from her own Social Security account. Helen can only take benefits from one account, so she must choose which account to take benefits from: $450 from her own account, $300 from George's account, or $375 from Ken's account. Obviously, she would take benefits from her own account, which would pay her $450 per month.

What happens when Ken dies? Helen would be entitled to widow's benefits because:

- Ken was entitled to Social Security benefits.

- They were married for ten years before the divorce became final.

- Helen is age 60 or over (or is between the ages of 50 and 60 and disabled).

- Helen is not married.

- Helen is not entitled to a retirement benefit that is equal to or greater than Ken's benefit.

Marci also gets widow's benefits if she meets these requirements.

A widow's remarriage after age 60 will not prevent her from being entitled to widow's benefits on her prior deceased husband's earnings.

A widow's remarriage before age 60 will prevent her from receiving widow's benefits unless the subsequent marriage ends, whether by death, divorce, or annulment. If the subsequent marriage ends, the widow may become entitled or re-entitled to benefits on the prior deceased spouse's earnings beginning with the month the subsequent marriage ends.

As an example, assume that Maude's first husband died. At age 58, she met a wonderful widower and wanted to get remarried, but she realized that she would lose her entitlement to all of her deceased spouse's Social Security benefits when she turned age 60. This may explain why many senior citizens are living together unmarried.

If you receive a pension from government employment that was not covered by Social Security, then any Social Security benefits you receive based on your spouse's Social Security contributions (either as a spouse, widow, or widower) will be reduced by two-thirds of your government pension. Thus, the Social Security benefit is reduced $2 for every $3 of the government pension.

For example, assume Al received a monthly civil service pension of $600. He is also eligible for Social Security benefits based on his ex-wife's earnings. His Social Security benefit based on her earnings is $200 (one-third of Al's civil service pension). There are some exceptions; if you have a client that receives a civil service pension, look up the rules on the Social Security website.

OTHER SOCIAL SECURITY ISSUES

- Discovery requests should include the Social Security Administration report, which discloses past earnings and anticipated benefits of the ex-spouse.

- Social Security benefits are not a marital asset subject to division. However, a judge may consider the anticipated benefits as a factor in dividing marital assets.

- Less than full benefits can be paid as early as age 62, but monthly benefit amounts will be permanently reduced if taken early.

- Since the primary claimant of Social Security would receive 100% of the benefit at full retirement, and the ex-spouse would receive only 50% of the benefit, alimony can be used to equalize the benefits.

- Clients should be advised to keep information regarding their ex-spouse's Social Security numbers, date and place of birth, and names of parents.

- They should also be informed regarding their ex-spouse's death to make sure that they are getting their full Social Security benefits.

- Even if the wage-earner spouse defers receiving his or her benefits until age 70, the ex-spouse may elect to receive benefits at age 62 or full retirement age.

- Clients should be advised to apply for retirement benefits in a timely fashion. Unclaimed earlier benefits are lost forever; there is no "back pay." However, benefits would be paid out at a higher monthly rate if the client waits until age 70; the benefits would not be paid out at a higher rate if they wait until after age 70. Darlene waited until age 71 to apply for Social Security benefits. She will receive a higher payout because she waited until age 70 to claim her benefits. However, the payout is no higher, other than for cost of living increases, at age 71 than the benefits would have been at age 70. As a result, Darlene lost a whole year of benefits without a corresponding increase in the monthly benefit.

- Social Security benefits paid to a parent are includible in a parent's gross income for purposes of calculating child support.

- When Social Security payments are paid for the benefit of the child (derivative benefits) due to the parents disability or retirement, in most states, there is a rebuttable presumption that these Social Security payments should be credited as child support from that parent because it is due to that parent's prior earnings. This issue should be specified in the settlement agreement. The presumption may be different if the Social Security is paid due to the child's disability.

- A valid prenuptial agreement cannot waive either party's right to apply for and receive Social Security benefits.

- A spouse qualifies for benefits if the marriage is either legal, a common law marriage, or a deemed marriage, such as when in good faith a person went through a marriage ceremony that would have been valid, but there was some legal impediment.

- Widow(er)'s benefits can be applied for at age 60 if there is no remarriage before age 60. A surviving spouse or former spouse may want to consider delaying remarriage until he or she is 60 years old and the benefits are in pay status.

- Advise clients to be diligent about notifying the Social Security Administration about name changes to ensure that they are receiving credit for withholding.

CHAPTER 7
INSURANCE

Learning Objectives

After completing this chapter, you will be able to:

1. Explain health insurance and benefits provided by the Consolidated Omnibus Budget Reconciliation Act (COBRA).
2. Recognize the issues surrounding life insurance coverage and divorce.

It is important to review your clients' current insurance coverage and how that coverage will change once the divorce is final. What are the options for insurance after the divorce?

HEALTH INSURANCE AND COBRA

In the traditional marriage where the husband is the main wage earner, one concern is maintaining health insurance for the ex-wife after divorce.

It is not uncommon for women over 40 to develop severe health problems. Some become almost uninsurable, at least at a reasonable cost. This is a real concern when, all of a sudden, they are on their own and responsible for acquiring health insurance.

The Consolidated Omnibus Budget Reconciliation Act (COBRA) law was passed in 1986 to help women who are divorcing. It allows women to continue to get health insurance from their ex-husband's company if it has at least 20 employees, for three years after the divorce. The normal COBRA provision states that, if an employee is fired or leaves a job, he or she can get health insurance from that company for 18 months. However, in a divorce, it is extended to three years or 36 months.

Assume that Sara decides to continue health insurance under COBRA. Sara must pay the premium as agreed. If she misses a premium payment, the health insurance company can drop her and they do not need to reinstate her. It is imperative for the ex-spouse to pay the premium on time. Typically, Sara will not get the discounted group rate but will be charged the full rate. It is important to shop for health insurance. Even though COBRA may be the best option to maintain health insurance in the short term, it may not be the best option long term. The ex-spouse may be able to purchase health insurance at a lesser cost somewhere else.

It is important to discuss health insurance options with your clients. A client, healthy or not, may decide that they are going to get coverage from their ex-spouse's COBRA. They should be told about the risk of developing health problems during the COBRA coverage and subsequently being unable to find reasonably priced health insurance after the COBRA coverage expires.

Encourage clients over age 40 to explore other options. They should be advised to shop for health insurance. If you can match the COBRA rate from your ex-spouse's company or get a lower premium with another company, you should buy your own. Then if something happens, as long as you pay your premiums, you are covered. Otherwise, at the end of three years, COBRA drops you, and then you have to start shopping for your own insurance, which could be costly.

Is health insurance a marital asset? Some companies provide health benefits for employees after they retire. Some lawyers are starting to consider this an asset since the Financial Accounting Standards Board in 1993 began requiring employers to calculate the present value of the future benefits and show a liability for that value in their financial reports.

LIFE INSURANCE

It is important to review life insurance coverage during the divorce process.

Spousal support generally stops upon the death of the payor. However, the stream of payments can be covered using life insurance on the life of the payor if there are no other adequate sources of security for the future stream of income. Insurance is a way to cover any cash flow shortage and should be part of the final divorce settlement.

If insurance is required as part of the judgment, then the recipient spouse should own the life insurance policy and make the premium payments. This prevents any changes in the policy without his or her knowledge.

Here is an example. Joan was receiving $400 per month in spousal support from her ex-husband, Jerry. The court ordered Jerry to carry life insurance on his life payable to Joan as long as spousal support was being paid. After three years, Jerry was tired of making the insurance payments so he stopped and the insurance was canceled. Nobody knew about it until Jerry was in a car accident and died two weeks later of complications from his injuries. Joan's spousal support came to an abrupt halt and there was no life insurance! Yes, Jerry was in contempt of court, but it was too late to make up for the life insurance death benefit because his estate was insufficient to pay Joan's claim.

It may also be advisable to build cash value within the policy. Then, the cash account within the policy is hers and she may even use it for retirement. She can borrow from it at any time or cancel the policy and use the cash.

Another option would be to purchase level term insurance for the duration of the spousal support if the wife cannot afford premium payments. She could "buy term and invest the difference" in a mutual fund that she can manage.

A third recommendation is to apply for any insurance required pursuant to the terms of the divorce before the divorce is final. Then, if the husband cannot pass the physical and cannot get new insurance, there is still time to modify the final settlement to make up for this possibility.

If the court orders the husband to purchase insurance to cover spousal support and the wife owns the policy, those premium payments are treated like spousal support for tax purposes and he can deduct them from his taxable income. Likewise, the wife will need to declare them as taxable income, unless the parties agree in their separation agreement to exempt the payments from the spousal support tax treatment.

Is term insurance ever considered a marital asset? Yes, in some states, if the insured has since become uninsurable, the insurance could be considered an asset. It is something that should be considered.

CHAPTER 8
DEBT, CREDIT, AND BANKRUPTCY

Learning Objectives

After completing this chapter, you will be able to:

1. Classify debt as "marital" or "separate."
2. Differentiate between secured and unsecured debt.
3. Discuss how to help clients avoid potential future tax liabilities.
4. Define qualified principal residence indebtedness.
5. Recognize divorce-related expenses.
6. List the types of credit: joint accounts and potential liability post-divorce.
7. Explain the complexities of divorce and bankruptcy.

DEBT

As you read earlier, property is classified as marital and separate. The same classifications apply to debt. In general, both parties are responsible for any debts incurred during the marriage. It does not matter who really spent the money. When the property is divided during the divorce, the spouse that receives the asset is generally also responsible for any loans secured by that asset.

It is in your client's best interest to pay off as many debts as possible before or at the time of the final decree. To do so, clients could use liquid assets such as bank accounts, stocks, or bonds. It may make sense to sell assets to accumulate some extra cash. The best assets to sell include extra cars, vacation homes, and excess furniture.

If the parties cannot pay off their debts, then the decree must state which spouse will pay each debt and when each debt will be paid. *However, both parties are still personally liable to the third-party creditor regardless of what the court order says.*

There are generally four types of debt to consider: secured debt, unsecured debt, tax debt, and divorce expense debt.

SECURED DEBT

Secured debt includes the mortgage on the house or other real estate and loans on cars, trucks, and other vehicles. It should be made very clear in the separation agreement which party will pay each debt. If one spouse fails to make a payment on a debt that is secured by an asset, the creditor can pursue payment from the other spouse or repossess or foreclose on the secured asset.

UNSECURED DEBT

Unsecured debt includes credit cards, personal bank loans, lines of credit, and loans from parents and friends. These debts may be divided equitably. The court also considers who is better able to pay the debt, in the context of the full financial settlement.

For unsecured debt, the separation agreement needs to include a hold-harmless clause. In most cases, this will indemnify the non-paying spouse, which means that the paying spouse gives the non-paying spouse the right to collect all missed payments and, in some cases, also damages, interest, and attorneys' fees if payments were not made.

Financial advisors, lawyers, and clients all should be aware that even though something is agreed to and included in the divorce decree, it does not mean that it will happen as planned. Often, the legal decision and the financial outcome are very different things.

Here is an example. Tracy and Paul were married for eight years; during that time, Tracy ran their credit card to the limit with her compulsive spending. The court held Tracy solely responsible for paying the $12,000 in credit card debt. After the divorce, however, Tracy did not change her ways and was unable to pay off her debt. The credit card companies came after Paul, who ended up paying them off. One solution would have been to pay off the credit cards with assets at the time of the divorce or for Paul to have received additional property to offset this possibility.

TAX DEBT

Just because the divorce settlement is final does not mean the parties are exempt from possible future tax liability. For three years after the divorce, the IRS can perform a random audit of joint tax returns. In addition, the IRS can audit a joint return—if it has good cause to do so—for seven years. It can also audit a return whenever it feels fraud is involved.

To avoid potential tax liability, the divorce agreement should provide for what happens if any additional interest, penalties, or taxes are assessed, as well as where the money comes from to pay for costs incurred to hire professionals if there is an audit.

Remember, if a joint tax return was filed, each party is individually responsible to the IRS unless a spouse qualifies under the innocent spouse regulations.

QUALIFIED PRINCIPAL RESIDENCE INDEBTEDNESS

The tax code provides that if debt is discharged (forgiven) by the lender, the lender generally has to report the amount of the debt discharged as income to the debtor with a 1099. However, you can temporarily exclude canceled debt from income if it is qualified principal residence indebtedness. It applies for debt that is canceled in calendar years 2007 through 2014. Qualified principal residence indebtedness is any debt (up to $2 million) incurred in acquiring, constructing, or substantially improving your principal residence and is secured by your principal residence. Qualified principal residence indebtedness also includes any debt secured by your principal residence resulting from the refinancing of debt incurred to acquire, construct, or substantially improve your principal residence, but only to the extent the amount of debt does not exceed the amount of the refinanced debt. The debt that is excluded from income under this provision must reduce the basis (but not below zero) of the residence.

DIVORCE EXPENSES

Your clients will incur costs during the divorce process, including court filing fees, appraisals, mediation fees, and legal fees. Other less obvious expenses are accounting, financial planning, and counseling. The separation agreement should state who is responsible for these expenses.

There are also divorce expenses that may accrue after the final decree, such as attorney fees for doing QDROs and title transfers. Other post-decree expenses are tax preparation for the final joint tax return, mediation fees, and long-term divorce counseling for the parents or the children. Who pays? The attorney should spell it out clearly so there are no disputes at a later date.

CREDIT

A creditor cannot close an account just because the account holder's marital status has changed. An exception would be if there was a proven inability or unwillingness to pay. However, the creditor can require a new application if the original application was based solely on the other spouse's financial statement. The creditor must allow use of the account while the new application is being reviewed.

If the spouses have joint charge accounts, they will both have the same credit history. If one spouse merely used the accounts as a signee, it may be necessary to confirm the fact that he or she was equally responsible for the payments. This can be done with proof of canceled checks and a financial statement that shows that spouse's ability to pay.

If your client has a good credit history and the necessary income, he or she should have little or no problem opening new accounts solely in his or her name. If, however, the client was unemployed during the marriage and never had a credit card in his or her name, he or she may need a cosigner.

Your client may still be responsible for joint accounts even after the divorce is final. Prior to issuance of the final decree, all joint accounts should be paid off and closed, and each spouse, if they desire, can open new accounts.

Clients should be warned not to run up charge accounts as part of divorce planning or retaliation. If it is proven that both spouses did not agree to these expenditures or they were not for necessities such as food, housing, clothing, or health care, then they may not be considered joint debt depending on state law and the facts of the case.

NOTE: Creditors do not care how the separation agreement divides responsibility for the debt. Each person is liable for the full amount of the debt on joint accounts until the bill is paid.

BANKRUPTCY

The word bankruptcy strikes fear in the hearts of many people – especially those going through a divorce. Many wives who are trying to decide whether it is better to ask for spousal support or a property settlement note are caught in a dilemma. Perhaps the husband has threatened to leave the country if he has to pay spousal support. Another common threat is to file for bankruptcy to avoid paying a property settlement note. Here is an overview of the bankruptcy rules as they apply in a divorce case.

There are two types of bankruptcy available:

- Chapter 13 allows you to develop a pay-off plan over a three-year period. The assets may be preserved and the debtor is allowed to pay off all of the secured debt, as well as a portion of the unsecured debt, and discharge the rest of the unsecured debt. The debtor needs to make payments under a plan.

- Chapter 7 allows you to liquidate all of your assets and use the proceeds to pay off your debts, erasing the debts that cannot be paid in full. All unsecured debts are forgiven, and all assets over statutory minimum protected amounts are forfeited. Creditors have the right to repossess their fair share of the assets. The net proceeds from the sale of the assets are divided pro rata among the unsecured creditors.

Here are some things to remember:

- If a spouse files bankruptcy before, during, or after divorce, the creditors will seek out the other spouse for payment, no matter what was agreed to in the separation agreement.

- While the couple is still married, they can file for bankruptcy jointly. This will eliminate all separate debts of the husband, separate debts of the wife, and all jointly incurred marital debts.

Certain debts cannot be discharged in bankruptcy. These include child support, spousal support, some student loans, and recent taxes.

Promissory notes or property settlement notes, especially unsecured notes, are almost always wiped out in bankruptcy. Some secured notes, depending on the property that secures them, can also be discharged.

As an example, say Sam and Trudy agreed on how they were going to divide all of their assets. However, to achieve a 50/50 division, Sam was going to owe Trudy $82,000. Sam signed a property settlement note to pay Trudy the $82,000 over ten years at 5% interest. After the divorce, Sam filed for bankruptcy and listed the property settlement note as one of his debts. Trudy never received a penny of the $82,000.

SAMPLE TEST
QUESTIONS AND ANSWERS

After reading this module, complete all 100 sample test questions, grade your sample test, and read the answers and explanations. The questions and answers in this chapter will help you to learn and understand the material covered in this module and prepare for the actual exam.

1. After being married for 12 years, Marty and Madeleine are getting a divorce. Marty has a universal life insurance policy with a death benefit of $100,000 and a cash value of $10,000. Marty also has a ten-year term policy with a death benefit of $100,000. Both of these policies were purchased during the marriage and Madeleine is the beneficiary on both policies. What is the asset value of all of the insurance?

   a) $0
   b) $10,000
   c) $100,000
   d) $200,000

2. Which of the following is something a spouse should NOT consider when going through a divorce?

   a) What is our property?
   b) What is our property worth?
   c) How do we divide our property?
   d) How can I hide assets from my spouse?

3. Marital property is best defined as which of the following?

   a) It is brought into the marriage.
   b) It is inherited during the marriage.
   c) It is received as a gift during the marriage.
   d) It is earned during the marriage.

4. During Tammy's marriage, she received gifts that included two rings, some books, an antique dresser, and $2,000 from her mother. She put the $2,000 into a joint account with her mother. Which assets are considered Tammy's separate property?

    a) Two rings, some books, and an antique dresser
    b) Two rings, some books, an antique dresser, and $2,000
    c) $0
    d) $2,000

5. Many states would consider property to be marital property if it had which of the following attributes?

    a) It increased in value and was maintained as separate property.
    b) It was brought into the marriage and maintained as separate property.
    c) It was inherited and maintained as separate property.
    d) It was a gift and was maintained as separate property.

6. Which of the following is NOT a way a person could try to hide assets from his or her spouse?

    a) Deny the existence of an asset.
    b) Transfer assets to a third party.
    c) Create false debt.
    d) Set up an account in his or her spouse's name.

7. To discover hidden assets, a CDFA professional should review tax returns going back how many years?

    a) One
    b) Three
    c) Five
    d) Seven

8. When one spouse wants to continue living in the marital home, which factor is the least important to consider?

    a) Whether the spouse is emotionally tied to the house
    b) If there are minor children from the marriage living in the house
    c) Whether the spouse can afford to continue living in the house
    d) What the financial impact on the spouse would be

9. Which of the following is a risk that a retired participant may face with his or her pension (defined benefit plan) in a divorce?

    a) Double dipping
    b) Vesting
    c) Forfeiture
    d) QDRO limitations

10. Which of the following is not required to be included in a Qualified Domestic Relations Order (QDRO)?

    a) Name of the plan
    b) Address of the participant
    c) The amount of the benefit
    d) The name of the alternate payee's attorney

11. Nicole, age 48, has been married to Andy for 12 years and has worked for her current company for 19 years. She has received a statement from her company stating that based upon her current years of service and income, she is eligible to receive $1,900 per month at age 65 from her defined benefit plan. Assuming an interest rate of 5%, what is the present value of the marital portion of her plan?

    a) $72,639
    b) $115,013
    c) $166,001
    d) $263,611

12. Which of the following schedules on a tax return will NOT help the CDFA professional find hidden assets?

    a) Schedule C
    b) Schedule D
    c) Schedule E
    d) Schedule H

13. Which of the following should a CDFA professional review in addition to the spouses' tax returns?

   a) Social Security numbers on the return
   b) Charitable contribution receipts
   c) W-2s and 1099s
   d) Tax returns from previous spouses

14. Which of the following strategies can a CDFA professional suggest to a client to help preserve assets during a divorce?

   a) Make purchases on joint credit cards.
   b) Transfer assets to family members.
   c) Set up bank accounts in a child's name.
   d) Reduce unnecessary expenses.

15. Which of the following resources is NOT useful to discover the existence of unknown or forgotten assets and liabilities?

   a) Mortgage closing documents for the family home
   b) Tax returns
   c) Paystubs
   d) Monthly mortgage statements for the family home

16. Greg and Marsha are getting a divorce. Greg began contributing to his 401(k) plan before he married Marsha. He has been contributing $1,000 per month to his 401(k) and he has $400,000 in it. What kind of property is the 401(k)?

   a) It is separate property because he started contributing before the marriage.
   b) It is separate property because it is in his name and it came directly from his wages.
   c) It is all marital property because he has been contributing during the marriage.
   d) It is marital and separate property because he started contributing before the marriage.

17. Which of the following is NOT a career asset?

   a) Job experience
   b) A car paid for out of employee paychecks
   c) Vacation and sick pay
   d) Employer-provided golf club membership

18. Which state is essentially a community property state, but has exceptions to the typical community property rules?

   a) Iowa
   b) Louisiana
   c) Minnesota
   d) Wisconsin

19. Which state is a community property state?

   a) Alabama
   b) Idaho
   c) Oklahoma
   d) Oregon

20. Which statement best sums up the belief that an ex-spouse deserves enough spousal support to maintain his or her lifestyle and nothing more?

   a) "Enough is enough"
   b) "Enough is more than enough"
   c) "Lifestyle support"
   d) "Rehabilitative maintenance"

21. Which of the following statements best describes how assets are split in a divorce?

   a) All states require an equal split of assets.
   b) All states require an equitable split of assets.
   c) Community property states generally require an equal split of assets.
   d) Community property states generally require an equitable split of assets.

22. Which of the following is true about community property status?

    a) It can be purged by moving to an equitable distribution state for one year.
    b) It can be purged by filing for divorce in an equitable distribution state.
    c) Property cannot be purged of its community property status.
    d) It cannot be purged unless the court in the originating community property state consents.

23. Which of the following is a true statement regarding property settlement notes?

    a) They do not impose interest on the payor.
    b) They can qualify as spousal support for tax purposes.
    c) They can be collateralized with a QDRO.
    d) They are completely taxable.

24. Steve and Heidi agreed to divide their assets equally. Heidi is taking the home, car, and furniture, and Steve is taking his 401(k) and a rental property. What would the financial impact be after five years?

    a) Heidi's working capital would absolutely be higher than Steve's.
    b) Steve's working capital would absolutely be higher than Heidi's.
    c) Heidi's net worth would probably be higher than Steve's.
    d) Steve's net worth would probably be higher than Heidi's.

25. Which of the following individuals should appraise a business that is part of the marital property?

    a) An in-house CPA
    b) A CPA with no ties to the business
    c) A qualified appraiser
    d) A CDFA professional

26. Which of the following is NOT a common option for the disposition of a business that is part of the marital property?

    a) One spouse keeps the business.
    b) Both spouses keep the business.
    c) They sell the business.
    d) They gift the business to the children.

27. Which of the following best describes an equitable property settlement?

    a) It is the same as an equal property settlement.

    b) It is not the same as an equal property settlement.

    c) It is when the parties divide the marital property 50/50.

    d) It is used in a community property state to divide marital property.

28. When assets are rolled over from a qualified retirement plan to an IRA, what percentage of taxes is the plan administrator required to withhold?

    a) 0%

    b) 10%

    c) 20%

    d) 25%

29. Which of the following is a characteristic of defined benefit plans?

    a) They have cash value today.

    b) They have no cash value today.

    c) They issue statements that show the value of the accounts.

    d) They have no survivor benefits.

30. Which of the following uses vesting schedules?

    a) Property settlement notes

    b) Defined contribution plans

    c) IRAs

    d) Mutual funds

31. If Bob contributes $1,000 to his retirement plan and then quits or is fired, what happens to his retirement plan?

    a) Bob will forfeit the $1,000 if he is not vested.

    b) Bob can take the $1,000.

    c) Bob can take the $1,000 if he quit, but not if he was fired.

    d) Bob can take the $1,000 as a distribution and pay no tax or penalty.

32. Dave contributes $1,000 to his retirement plan and his employer contributes $1,000 to the plan. If Dave quits and he is 60% vested, what amount is his?

    a) $1,000
    b) $1,200
    c) $1,600
    d) $2,000

33. If Kurt takes a distribution out of his retirement plan before he is 59 ½, which of the following will occur?

    a) Kurt will always pay a tax penalty on the distribution.
    b) Kurt may pay a tax penalty on the distribution.
    c) Kurt will never pay a tax penalty on the distribution.
    d) Kurt cannot take a distribution before age 59 ½.

34. When a distribution is paid from a qualified retirement plan, what is the percentage of taxes that the plan administrator must withhold?

    a) 0%
    b) 10%
    c) 20%
    d) 25%

35. When a distribution is paid from an IRA, the trustee must withhold what percentage of taxes?

    a) 0%
    b) 10%
    c) 20%
    d) 25%

36. If a qualified retirement plan is being transferred to a non-participant spouse pursuant to a QDRO, payment of a tax penalty can be avoided if a distribution is taken by the:

    a) Participant spouse within six years from the date the divorce becomes final.
    b) Non-participant spouse within six years from the date the divorce becomes final.
    c) Participant spouse as a one-time opportunity.
    d) Non-participant spouse as a one-time opportunity.

37. What is the tax penalty for taking an early distribution from a retirement plan?

   a) 0%
   b) 10%
   c) 20%
   d) 25%

38. Joe and Barb, both age 52, are divorcing and have agreed to split Joe's 401(k) equally. The value of the 401(k) is $200,000. Barb had the plan administrator transfer $80,000 to her IRA and distribute $20,000 directly to Barb. Which of the following will occur as a result of this distribution?

   a) Barb will not have to pay ordinary income tax or a tax penalty.
   b) Barb will not have to pay ordinary income tax, but she will pay a tax penalty on the $20,000.
   c) Barb will pay ordinary income tax on $20,000, but will not pay a tax penalty.
   d) Barb will pay ordinary income tax on $100,000, but will only pay a tax penalty on $20,000.

39. Which of the following is NOT a true statement regarding survivor benefits from a pension plan?

   a) The QDRO needs to state that the spouses are taking the joint and survivor annuity option.
   b) The plan administrator will assume that the spouses are taking the joint and survivor annuity option unless told otherwise.
   c) The non-participant spouse can have his or her portion of the pension set up as a separate account.
   d) The QDRO should address the survivor benefits.

40. If the plan administrator transfers the retirement assets directly to the IRA trustee, which of the following will occur upon the transfer?

   a) There will be withholding.
   b) There will be no withholding.
   c) There will be income tax but no tax penalty.
   d) There will be income tax and a tax penalty.

41. Which of the following accounts will NOT issue statements with the current account value?

    a) IRAs
    b) Defined benefit plans
    c) Defined contribution plans
    d) Brokerage accounts

42. Which of the following methods of dividing pension benefits allows the court to decide how to divide the pension at some point in the future?

    a) Present value
    b) Deferred division
    c) Reserved jurisdiction
    d) Cash-out method

43. Which of the following assets promises to pay the owner a certain amount per month at retirement time?

    a) Defined benefit plan
    b) Defined contribution plan
    c) Traditional IRA
    d) Roth IRA

44. Which of the following methods of dividing pension benefits should be a last resort?

    a) Present value
    b) Deferred division
    c) Reserved jurisdiction
    d) Cash-out method

45. A QDRO is used as a means to divide which of the following?

    a) A traditional IRA by giving the non-participant spouse a two-thirds share
    b) A Roth IRA equally between the two spouses
    c) A non-qualified stock option equally between the two spouses
    d) A 401(k) by giving the non-participant spouse a two-thirds share

46. Which of the following is the biggest detriment if one owns a 401(k) plan versus a company pension?

    a) Risk for employer mismanagement of the retirement funds
    b) Potential financial demise of the employer
    c) Absence of any cost of living increase
    d) No ability to take distributions prior to retirement

47. The numerator of the coverture fraction is the total number of years:

    a) Worked until retirement
    b) Married while working
    c) Single while working
    d) Worked until the divorce is final

48. When will some companies allow the ex-spouse to start receiving pension benefits?

    a) At the participant's earliest retirement age, even if the participant has not retired.
    b) As soon as the QDRO has been accepted, regardless of either party's age.
    c) At the non-participant's retirement age.
    d) No company will allow benefits to be paid until the employee retires.

49. Tim, age 38, has worked for his company for 16 years. He has decided to divorce Erin after an 18-year marriage. His company says he is eligible for full retirement at age 62 and will receive $2,800 per month based on his current years of service and income. Assuming an interest rate of 4.8%, what is the present value of the marital portion of his plan?

    a) $105,897
    b) $118,986
    c) $326,255
    d) $366,578

50. Jim, age 52, has worked for his company for 20 years and is planning to retire at age 65 on a pension that will pay him $2,150 per month based on his current years of service and income. The benefit will not increase for inflation. He has been married to his current wife for 17 years. Assuming an interest rate of 5.4%, what is the present value of the marital portion of his plan?

    a) $109,336
    b) $128,631
    c) $216,617
    d) $254,844

51. Mike, age 54, has been married for 28 years. He has also worked for his current company for 28 years. He received a statement from his company stating that based on his current years of service and income, he is eligible to receive $2,600 per month at age 62 from his defined benefit plan. His plan is protected from inflation. Assuming an interest rate of 6% and an inflation rate of 3%, what is the present value of the marital portion of his plan?

    a) $211,466
    b) $267,308
    c) $337,046
    d) $426,048

52. Which of the following employee benefits must be transferred to an alternate payee with a QDRO?

    a) Accrued sick pay
    b) Life insurance
    c) Disability insurance
    d) 401(k) plan

53. What does a QDRO do?

    a) It only tells the administrator how the assets in the plan are to be divided.
    b) It only tells the administrator what happens to the qualified assets if either party dies.
    c) It only tells the trustee what happens to the IRA assets when either party dies.
    d) It tells the administrator both how the assets in the plan are to be divided and what happens to the assets if either party dies.

54. When did the QDRO come into existence?

    a) 1974
    b) 1984
    c) 1986
    d) 1997

55. The denominator of the coverture fraction is the total number of years that the person:

    a) Worked until retirement
    b) Was married while working
    c) Was single while working
    d) Was married

56. Which of the following is NOT an option that should be recommended to a couple regarding their marital home?

    a) Sell the house and divide the proceeds from the sale.
    b) Have one spouse buy out the other spouse.
    c) Continue to own the home and sell it at a later date.
    d) Let the home go into foreclosure.

57. Wilma is transferring her interest in the marital residence to her former husband, Fred, by quitclaim deed. Which of the following will happen to the mortgage?

    a) She will automatically be released from liability for any mortgages on the residence.
    b) She will remain liable for the mortgage on the residence.
    c) The mortgage company will require Fred to refinance the mortgage.
    d) The mortgage company will immediately foreclose on the property.

58. Sally and Marty are divorcing. Sally is going to buy out Marty's interest in their marital home. Which of the following is typically the best way to accomplish this?

    a) Use a note payable between Sally and Marty.
    b) Require Sally to refinance the mortgage and Marty takes another asset equal in value to the equity in the home.
    c) Continue with the same mortgage and have Sally make all of the remaining payments.
    d) Allocate Marty's 401(k) to him equal to the equity in the marital home; there will be no need to refinance.

59. If both spouses are going to continue to own the home jointly after the divorce, although only one of them will continue to live in the house, then the resident spouse should pay 100% of which of the following expenses?

    a) Mortgage payments
    b) Major repairs
    c) Improvements
    d) Minor repairs

60. Adam and Kim are divorced. Adam was awarded use of their jointly-owned home for three years. It has been three years and Adam and Kim have sold the home for $920,000. The basis was $360,000, the mortgage was $420,000, and the selling expenses were $35,000. What is Kim's taxable capital gain?

    a) $0
    b) $12,500
    c) $30,000
    d) $262,500

61. Which of the following is NOT considered to calculate the cost basis of the family home?

    a) The purchase price of the house
    b) The closing costs on the purchase of the house
    c) Any repairs made to the house
    d) Any improvements made to the house

62. What amount of gain can single taxpayers generally exclude upon the sale of their principal residence?

    a) $250,000
    b) $250,000 plus any mortgage balances
    c) $500,000
    d) $500,000 plus any mortgage balances

63. Steve and Lori have a home worth $560,000. They bought it when they got married 25 years ago for $185,000. They refinanced their mortgage several years ago and the current mortgage is $420,000. Lori decided to keep the home. She later decides to sell it with 5% sales costs. Using today's value, what is the amount of taxable gain Lori will report on her tax return?

    a) $0
    b) $97,000
    c) $125,000
    d) $347,000

64. How often can the exclusion from capital gains tax upon the sale of the principal residence generally be used?

    a) Every two years
    b) Every three years
    c) Every four years
    d) Every five years

65. If the non-working spouse is more than 60 years old and has limited assets but wants to keep the house, what is the best way to handle the house post-divorce?

    a) Keep the house only if it is paid off.
    b) Keep the house regardless of whether it is paid off.
    c) Keep the house only if it would cost more to rent something else.
    d) Under no circumstances should he or she keep the house.

66. John owned his home for two years prior to marrying Linda. John and Linda just divorced after only one year of marriage. John transferred his interest in the residence to Linda pursuant to the terms of the divorce. Three months later, Linda received an offer to purchase the home for $800,000. Linda lived in the home for one year and three months; John lived in the home for three years. John paid $350,000 for the home, which was worth $750,000 when they divorced. How will any capital gains on the sale of the marital residence be reported and in what amount?

   a) Linda will have to report a capital gain of $450,000.
   b) Linda will have to report a capital gain of $200,000.
   c) John will have to report a capital gain of $450,000.
   d) John will have to report a capital gain of $200,000.

67. Brett bought his house for $160,000 before he married Kelly. They put improvements into the house totaling $40,000. They also made some repairs around the house totaling $10,000. Kelly is getting the house, which is now worth $350,000. What is Kelly's cost basis of the house?

   a) $160,000
   b) $200,000
   c) $210,000
   d) $350,000

68. Which of the following factors is generally NOT considered when a judge awards spousal support?

   a) The property settlement
   b) The presence of minor children
   c) The length of marriage
   d) The income and resources of each spouse's parents

69. Which of the following does a judge generally consider when awarding child support?

   a) The need of one spouse
   b) The ability of one spouse to pay child support
   c) The age and health of both parties
   d) The child support guidelines

70. Sara has never worked and has $5,200 in monthly expenses. Her husband earns $265,000 per year. Sara is a candidate for spousal support in which of the following circumstances?

    a) She has been married for ten or more years.
    b) She has been getting $10,000 a month from a trust fund.
    c) She has minor children to care for.
    d) She has limited career options.

71. Which of the following would be appropriate criteria for a judge to use to determine the need for spousal support?

    a) The payor's expenses only
    b) The recipient's income only
    c) The recipient's expenses less the recipient's income
    d) The payor's income and ability to pay

72. Which of the following would be appropriate criteria for a judge to use to determine the ability to pay spousal support?

    a) The recipient's expenses only
    b) The payor's income only
    c) The recipient's expenses less the recipient's income
    d) The payor's income and ability to pay

73. Which of the following circumstances would trigger the recapture rules if spousal support ceases?

    a) The death of the recipient
    b) The death of the payor
    c) The remarriage of the recipient
    d) The cohabitation of the recipient

74. Tony, age 45, has been married to Dawn for 24 years and has worked for his current company for 21 years. Based on his current years of service and income, he is eligible to receive $2,850 per month at age 65 from his defined benefit plan that is protected from inflation. Assuming an interest rate of 5% and an inflation rate of 3%, what is the present value of the marital portion of his plan?

    a) $123,653
    b) $148,981
    c) $328,089
    d) $395,290

75. Rehabilitative maintenance provides which of the following types of financial help?

    a) Temporary if the recipient has a disability
    b) Permanent if the recipient has a child with a disability
    c) Temporary until the recipient is able to earn sufficient income
    d) Permanent unless the recipient is able to earn sufficient income

76. Which of the following would qualify as spousal support?

    a) Payments made to maintain property owned by the payor for the benefit of the ex-spouse
    b) Support payments for each child pursuant to a court order
    c) Support payments to the ex-spouse pursuant to a court order
    d) Support payments to the ex-spouse that both parties agreed to outside of the judgment for divorce

77. Sara asks Mike to paint her house in lieu of one month's spousal support payment of $800. Which of the following statements is true?

    a) Mike can deduct $800 as spousal support.
    b) Mike has complied with the order for payment of spousal support.
    c) Mike cannot deduct $800 as spousal support.
    d) Mike can deduct $800 as spousal support only if Sara claims it as income.

78. Jane asks her ex-husband George to pay her additional spousal support in the amount of $500 until she finds a new job. Which of the following is the tax treatment of the payment?

    a) George can deduct the extra $500 if Jane agrees.
    b) George must deduct the extra $500.
    c) George cannot deduct the extra $500.
    d) George can deduct the extra $500 if Jane claims it as income.

79. If Mary's divorce was final on December 18, 2014, what is her filing status for 2014?

    a) She can file a joint return with her ex-husband.
    b) She can file as single only.
    c) She can file as head of household only.
    d) She can file as either single or head of household, depending on her circumstances.

80. Keith was ordered to pay Cindy spousal support for five years. They have two children. Which of the following scenarios will trigger the recapture rules?

    a) When payments drop by $15,000 in year two and by $15,000 in year three
    b) When payments drop by $15,000 in year three
    c) When payments drop by $25,000 in year four due to a child-related contingency
    d) When payments drop by $15,000 in year three and by $15,000 in year five, when each of their children reaches age 21

81. Recapture applies in which of the following situations?

    a) If spousal support ends due to the death of either spouse
    b) If spousal support declines because it is based on a percentage of the income earned by the payor-spouse
    c) If spousal support has declined by $20,000 in year three
    d) If spousal support has declined by $20,000 in year four

82. Which of the following describes the relationship between child support and maintenance and how child support changes?

    a) As maintenance increases, child support decreases.
    b) As maintenance decreases, child support decreases.
    c) As maintenance increases, child support increases.
    d) There is no relationship between child support and maintenance.

83. Which of the following is always modifiable?

    a) Child support
    b) Spousal support
    c) Property division
    d) Dissolution of the marriage

84. How often can the custodial parent transfer the tax exemption to the non-custodial parent?

    a) The tax exemption can only be transferred to the non-custodial parent for one year.
    b) The tax exemption can only be transferred to the non-custodial parent for more than one year.
    c) The tax exemption can be transferred to the non-custodial parent for one or more years.
    d) The tax exemption cannot be transferred to the non-custodial parent.

85. Which of the following is a true statement regarding the re-characterization of support?

    a) Spousal support can be re-characterized as child support if spousal support payments are reduced within one year before or after a child reaches the age of 18, 21, or the age of majority.
    b) Spousal support can be re-characterized as child support if spousal support payments are reduced within six months before or after a child reaches the age of 18, 21, or the age of majority.
    c) Child support can be re-characterized as spousal support if child support payments are reduced within one year before or after a child reaches the age of 18, 21, or the age of majority.
    d) Child support can be re-characterized as spousal support if child support payments are reduced within six months before or after a child reaches the age of 18, 21, or the age of majority.

86. The multiple-reduction rule applies when children are between 18 and 24 inclusively in which of the following situations?

   a) When there is more than one child and child support payments are reduced on two or more occasions
   b) When there is more than one child and spousal support payments are reduced on two or more occasions
   c) When there is a reduction of child support for one child on two or more occasions
   d) When there is a reduction of spousal support on two or more occasions

87. Margaret, who just turned age 65, was married first to Louis for 15 years and then to Harold for 12 years. She has not remarried since divorcing Harold. Louis, age 66, is receiving $1,250 per month from Social Security. Harold, age 67, is receiving $1,080 per month. Margaret has earned a benefit from Social Security of $820 per month. What is the highest Social Security benefit that Margaret is currently eligible to receive?

   a) $625
   b) $820
   c) $1,080
   d) $1,250

88. How many ex-spouses may collect on one worker's Social Security retirement benefits, assuming all other requirements are met?

   a) One
   b) Two
   c) Three
   d) Unlimited

89. Bob (age 65) and Sally (age 57) divorced after ten years of marriage. Bob received Social Security of $1,000 per month. Sally's Social Security benefit will be $750 per month at retirement. Bob died shortly after the divorce. How much will Sally be able to collect from Social Security at the time of Bob's death?

   a) $0
   b) $500
   c) $750
   d) $1,000

90. Gary works for an employer who has 20 or more employees. Following his divorce from Martha, how many months will Martha be eligible for COBRA insurance coverage?

    a) 12 months
    b) 18 months
    c) 24 months
    d) 36 months

91. When was The COBRA law passed?

    a) 1980
    b) 1986
    c) 1992
    d) 2000

92. Dave is ordered to pay lifetime spousal support and child support payments to his ex-wife, Sheila. Life insurance would be required in which of the following situations?

    a) To cover spousal and child support
    b) If the spouse requests it only
    c) To cover child support only
    d) If the judge requires it in his order

93. Life insurance is often a requirement in a divorce decree and should be obtained at which of the following times?

    a) As soon as the parties have an idea it is required
    b) When filing for the divorce
    c) After the divorce is final
    d) Only an existing policy should be used

94. Which of the following types of bankruptcy allows for the liquidation of all assets to pay off debt and then the remainder of the unpaid debt is forgiven?

    a) Chapter 7
    b) Chapter 11
    c) Chapter 12
    d) Chapter 13

95. Alex and Kim have a joint bank account with $25,000 in it, an ABC credit card with a balance of $2,500, and an XYZ credit card with a balance of $2,500. These are their only assets and debts. Which of the following divisions of assets and debts makes the most financial sense?

   a) They each take half the bank account and each takes over payments on one of the credit cards.
   b) Alex takes $15,000 from the bank account and he is responsible for both of the credit cards.
   c) Kim takes $15,000 from the bank account and she is responsible for both of the credit cards.
   d) They pay off the credit cards and each of them takes $10,000 from the bank account.

96. Matt and Claire have joint credit card debt of $8,000. Claire charged $6,000, and Matt charged $2,000 on the card. The divorce decree states that Matt will pay off the credit card debt. Who is liable for the debts?

   a) Matt is the only party liable for this debt.
   b) Matt is liable for $2,000, and Claire is liable for $6,000.
   c) Matt no longer has any liability for this debt.
   d) Matt and Claire are both liable for this debt.

97. Which of the following can be discharged in bankruptcy?

   a) Property settlement note
   b) Child support in arrears
   c) Spousal support in arrears
   d) Student loans

98. Gerald was ordered to carry life insurance to protect the lifetime spousal support he was paying to Madge. Which of the following options would offer Madge the LEAST protection?

   a) Gerald should transfer ownership of an existing policy to Madge.
   b) Madge should own the life insurance policy.
   c) Madge should be named as an irrevocable beneficiary on a policy owned by Gerald.
   d) Gerald should name Madge as the beneficiary on his life insurance at work.

99. In helping clients reach an equitable property settlement, which of the following should a CDFA professional consider?

    a) Only appreciating assets
    b) Only depreciating assets
    c) Both appreciating assets and depreciating assets
    d) Neither the anticipated appreciation nor depreciation of the assets

100. What does the Pension Benefit Guaranty Corporation (PBGC) do?

    a) Computes the present value of pensions
    b) Announces the monthly interest rates for the following month
    c) Drafts QDROs
    d) Requires income tax withholding from IRAs

ANSWERS TO SAMPLE TEST QUESTIONS

1. B; Page 2

   a) Only the term insurance has no value.
   b) **The cash value of life insurance is the asset value.**
   c) The death benefit is not included as the asset value.
   d) The death benefit is not included as the asset value.

2. D; Pages 1–3

   a) Both spouses should know what assets they own, including assets titled solely in one spouse's name.
   b) It is important to determine the value of the property.
   c) The divorce process will be shorter and less costly if the spouses can agree on how to divide their assets.
   d) **Hiding assets is unethical and may be illegal. Spouses should never be counseled to hide assets.**

3. D; Pages 2–3

   a) Property brought into the marriage is separate property.
   b) Property inherited during the marriage is separate property.
   c) Property received as a gift during the marriage is separate property.
   d) **Marital property is everything earned during the marriage even if it is kept in one spouse's name.**

4. B; Page 2

   a) Everything Tammy received as a gift is separate property.
   b) **Everything Tammy received as a gift, including the joint account with her mother, is separate property.**
   c) None of the gifts are marital property.
   d) The joint account is also Tammy's separate property.

5. A; Page 3

   a) **In some states, marital property also includes any increase in value of separate property.**

b) Real property brought into the marriage and maintained as separate property is not considered marital property.

c) Inherited property maintained as separate property is not considered marital property.

d) Property received as a gift and maintained as separate property is not considered marital property.

6. D; Page 3

a) Assets are sometimes hidden by denying the existence of an asset.

b) Assets are sometimes hidden by transferring a marital asset to a third party.

c) Assets are sometimes hidden by creating false debt.

d) **Setting up an account in the spouse's name to hide assets will not work very well.**

7. C; Page 3

a) It is not sufficient to look at only the past year's tax return as information that is needed may not be just in one year's statement.

b) It is not sufficient to look at tax returns for the past three years.

c) **It is recommended that one look at tax returns for the past five years because there may be assets that an individual is not aware of.**

d) Looking at tax returns for the past seven years would not be cost effective.

8. A; Page 42

a) **The primary consideration is whether the spouse can afford to keep the house; the emotional tie one has to the house is irrelevant.**

b) One factor to consider when one spouse wants to continue living in the marital home is if there are minor children from the marriage living in the home.

c) Another factor to consider when one spouse wants to continue living in the marital home is if that spouse can afford to continue living there.

d) Another factor to consider when one spouse wants to continue living in the marital home is to determine the financial impact of staying or leaving.

9. A; Page 32–33

a) **Sometimes a pension is divided as part of a property settlement. In some states, the income the employee receives from the pension is used to help** calculate spousal support or child support. This means that the recipient spouse gets paid twice from the same asset: he or she receives a share of the pension, then "double dips" by receiving support based on the participant's share of the pension income.

b) Vesting applies to defined contribution plans and is the proportion that an employee is entitled to from the retirement plan.

c) The retiree does not risk forfeiture of his or her pension.

d) The QDRO rules help the non-participant.

10. D; Page 37

a) The QDRO must include the name of the applicable plans.

b) The participant and alternate payee's last known addresses must be included.

c) Sufficient instruction to determine the amount of the benefit must be included.

d) **The name of the alternate payee's attorney does not have to be included in the QDRO.**

11. A; Pages 22–24

a) **See calculations below.**

Begin with 12/19 or 63% of the payments to determine the marital portion of the pension payments:

$$\left(\frac{12}{19}\right) x \ 1,900 = \$1,200$$

Nicole's life expectancy is 34.30 years, so she should live to be 82.30 years old.

Set your calculator for the beginning of the period (hit the blue button and the 7 key). Input the following data:

PMT = 1,200 *(monthly payment)*

n = 207.6 *(number of years between age 65 and 82.3, then multiplied by 12 months)*

i = .41667 *(interest rate divided by 12)*

FV = 0 *(enter 0 for the parameter you are not solving)*

Hit the PV (present value) button.

We find that the present value of the monthly payments is $166,491. That is the amount of money needed at age 65 to be able to pay Nicole $1,200 per month for 17.30 years, which is her life expectancy.

Now, calculate the present value as of today:

FV = 166,491

n = 17 *(number of years until she is 65)*

i = 5 *(interest rate)*

PMT = 0 *(there are no payments until she retires at age 65)*

Hit the PV (present value) button.

We find that the present value of the marital portion is **$72,639**.

b) This calculation used the full pension amount; it did not compute the marital share using the coverture fraction.
c) This is the present value at age 65, not the current value.
d) This is the present value at age 65 of the entire pension, not the marital share.

12. D; Page 4

a) Profit and loss from a business as reported on Schedule C may include depreciation expense which is not a cash outflow and should be added back to net income.
b) Capital gains and losses from the sale of stocks, bonds, and real estate are reported on Schedule D.
c) Income from rental properties, trusts, partnerships, and S-Corporations are reported on Schedule E, and depreciation would be something to review.
d) **Schedule H is used for household employment taxes.**

13. C; Page 4

a) A CDFA professional does not need to review Social Security numbers on a tax return.
b) A CDFA professional does not need to review charitable contribution receipts.
c) **A CDFA professional needs to review the 1099s and W-2s related to the tax return.**
d) A CDFA professional does not need to review tax returns from previous spouses.

14. D; Pages 3–5

a) A CDFA professional should not advise a client to make purchases on the joint credit card.
b) A CDFA professional should never advise a client to transfer assets to a family member to hide assets.
c) A CDFA professional should never advise a client to set up bank accounts in a child's name to hide assets.
d) **A CDFA professional should advise clients to reduce unnecessary expenses.**

15. D; Pages 3–5

a) Mortgage closing documents may disclose additional assets, debts, and income that the couple has.
b) Tax returns may disclose additional assets, debts, and income.
c) Paystubs may disclose additional assets, debts, and income, such as bonus compensation over and above base salary.
d) **The monthly mortgage statement only reveals the underlying property and the mortgage amount. It does not disclose any additional assets.**

16. D; Pages 2–3

a) Only those contributions Greg made before his marriage are separate property.
b) It is irrelevant that the 401(k) is in Greg's name or that he made contributions from his wages.
c) The contributions Greg made before his marriage are separate property.
d) **The contributions Greg made before his marriage are separate property; the contributions made during the marriage—and possibly the increase in value of the separate portion—are marital property.**

17. B; Pages 8–9

a) Job experience is a career asset.
b) **The family car is not a career asset.**
c) Vacation pay is a career asset.
d) An employer provided membership is a career asset.

18. D; Page 10

   a) Iowa is an equitable distribution state.
   b) Louisiana is a community property state.
   c) Minnesota is an equitable distribution state.
   d) **Wisconsin is essentially a community property state, but there are exceptions to the typical community property rules.**

19. B; Page 10

   a) Alabama is an equitable distribution state.
   b) **Idaho is a community property state.**
   c) Oklahoma is an equitable distribution state.
   d) Oregon is an equitable distribution state.

20. A; Page 10

   a) **The Wendt case broke through the long-held belief that "enough is enough," that a spouse deserved enough to maintain her lifestyle, but nothing more.**
   b) "Enough is more than enough" is not the correct theory.
   c) "Lifestyle support" is not the correct theory.
   d) "Rehabilitative maintenance" is used to support a spouse while he or she is getting back into the workforce.

21. C; Page 10

   a) Equitable distribution states do not require an equal split of assets.
   b) Community property states do not require an equitable split of assets.
   c) **Community property states require an equal split of assets.**
   d) Community property states do not use an equitable split of assets.

22. C; Page 10

   a) Property cannot be purged of its community property status by moving to an equitable distribution state.
   b) Property cannot be purged of its community property status by filing for divorce in an equitable distribution state.
   c) **Any property acquired in a community property state retains its community property status no matter where the couple moves.**

d) Property cannot be purged of its community property status even if the court in the community property state consents.

23. C; Page 12

 a) Interest may or may not be payable on a property settlement note.
 b) A property settlement note does not qualify as spousal support.
 c) **A property settlement note can be collateralized with a retirement plan using a QDRO.**
 d) Only the interest portion of the payment is taxable.

24. D; Pages 13–14

 a) Based on the assets Heidi selected, she is likely to have working capital lower than Steve's.
 b) Steve is likely to have a higher working capital than Heidi. It is not an absolute. Perhaps the house is in an area that is undergoing development and will appreciate significantly.
 c) Heidi has chosen assets that appreciate slowly or depreciate, and they take money to maintain.
 d) **Steve has chosen assets that generally increase in value or produce income. A few years after the divorce, Steve's net worth will likely exceed Heidi's and the gap will likely continue to widen.**

25. C; Page 14

 a) An in-house CPA should not be appraising a business where he or she works because he or she cannot be objective.
 b) A CPA without additional training is not sufficient to appraise the business.
 c) **It is imperative to have the business appraised by a qualified appraiser.**
 d) A CDFA professional without additional training is not sufficient to appraise the business.

26. D; Page 15

 a) Frequently, one spouse will keep the business and the other spouse will get other assets.
 b) Sometimes, both spouses will keep operating the business together. This may result in problems later on.
 c) Selling the business is a viable option.

    d) **Unless there is extreme wealth, giving away assets is not usually a financially viable option.**

27. B; Page 16

    a) "Equitable" does not necessarily mean "equal." It means "fair."

    b) **Equitable is not the same as an equal division of property.**

    c) Equitable is not a 50/50 division of property.

    d) Community property states use an equal division of property, not an equitable division.

28. A; Page 20

    a) **Assets that are rolled over directly from a qualified plan to an IRA avoid the withholding tax.**

    b) The 10% rate is the penalty for early distributions taken before the age of 59 ½.

    c) If this were a distribution to the alternate payee, then 20% would be required to be withheld for taxes.

    d) There is not a 25% withholding requirement.

29. B; Page 22

    a) A defined contribution plan has cash value today.

    b) **A defined benefit retirement plan promises to pay the employee a certain amount per month at retirement time; it has no cash value today.**

    c) They do not issue statements that show the value of the accounts.

    d) Some defined benefit plans have survivor benefits.

30. B; Page 18

    a) Property settlement notes do not have vesting schedules.

    b) **Defined contribution plans use vesting schedules.**

    c) IRAs are fully vested.

    d) Mutual funds do not use vesting schedules.

31. B; Page 18

    a) Bob is fully vested on his contributions.

    b) **Bob can take the amount he contributed ($1,000).**

    c) It does not matter if Bob quit or was fired; the $1,000 is his.

    d) Bob can take the $1,000, but he will pay tax and possibly a penalty if he takes it as a distribution.

32. C; Page 18

    a) Dave gets 100% of his contributions plus 60% of his employer's contributions ($600).

    b) Dave gets 100% of his contributions plus 60% of his employer's contributions ($600).

    c) **Dave can take the amount he contributed ($1,000) plus 60% of the $1,000 his employer contributed ($600).**

    d) Dave can take the $1,000 he contributed, but only 60% of the amount his employer contributed.

33. B; Page 19

    a) There are exceptions that allow someone to take distributions prior to age 59 ½ without paying the penalty.

    b) **Generally, a distribution made before a participant is age 59 ½ is an early distribution and subject to a 10% penalty. There are some exceptions to this rule.**

    c) Kurt will pay a penalty on the distribution if he does not meet one of the exceptions to the rule.

    d) Kurt can take a distribution prior to age 59 ½.

34. C; Page 20

    a) There is a 20% withholding requirement on any distribution taken from a qualified retirement account.

    b) The plan administrator is required to withhold 20% when distributions are taken from a qualified retirement account.

    c) **The Unemployment Compensation Amendment Act (UCA), which took effect in January 1993, states that any monies taken out of a qualified plan or tax-sheltered annuity are subject to 20% withholding.**

    d) There is a 20% withholding requirement on any distribution taken from a qualified retirement account.

35. A; Page 21

a) **An IRA is not considered a qualified plan and a distribution may take place without withholding 20% for taxes.**
b) There is no withholding requirement for IRAs.
c) There is no withholding requirement for IRAs; the 20% withholding is for distributions from qualified plans.
d) There is no withholding requirement for IRAs.

36. D; Page 19

a) The participant cannot take a distribution pursuant to IRC §72(t)(2)(C) and avoid the tax penalty.
b) The non-participant spouse is exempt from the penalty, pursuant to IRC §72(t)(2)(C), only if he or she takes the distribution prior to transferring the retirement assets to a separate account. Whether or not it is within six years is irrelevant.
c) It is the non-participant spouse that qualifies for a one-time distribution without paying a penalty.
d) **The non-participant spouse is exempt from the penalty, pursuant to IRC §72(t)(2)(C), if he or she takes a one-time distribution prior to transferring the retirement assets to a separate account.**

37. B; Page 19

a) The tax penalty for taking an early distribution is 10%.
b) **Generally, a distribution made before a participant is age 59 ½ is an early distribution and subject to a 10% penalty.**
c) The tax penalty for taking an early distribution is 10%.
d) The tax penalty for taking an early distribution is 10%.

38. C; Page 19

a) Barb will have to pay income tax on the distribution of $20,000.
b) Barb will not have to pay the penalty.
c) **Barb will pay income tax on the distribution, but no tax penalty because she qualified under IRC §72(t)(2)(C).**
d) Barb will not pay income tax on the amount transferred to her IRA nor a penalty on the distribution.

39. B; Page 31

    a) If the QDRO does not state that they are taking the joint and survivor annuity option, then they will lose that benefit.

    b) **The plan administrator will assume that the participant is taking the single life option unless instructed otherwise.**

    c) The non-participant spouse can have their part of the pension set up as a separate account.

    d) The QDRO should address the survivor benefits; otherwise, there will be none.

40. B; Page 20

    a) There is only withholding if there is a distribution to the participant or alternate payee.

    b) **There is no withholding tax when assets are transferred from a qualified plan to an IRA.**

    c) There will not be a tax or penalty because there was not a distribution.

    d) There will not be a tax or penalty because there was not a distribution.

41. B; Page 22

    a) The IRA owner will receive an account statement with the current value.

    b) **The value of a defined benefit plan comes from the company's guarantee to pay based on a predetermined plan formula. There is no account balance.**

    c) The defined contribution participant will receive an account statement with the current value.

    d) The owner of brokerage accounts will receive an account statement with the current value.

42. C; Pages 21–22

    a) The present value means that you use the present value of the income stream the participant is expecting to be paid, based on his earnings during the marriage. The non-participant spouse can either become an alternate payee or can be paid off out of some other marital assets.

    b) When deferred division is used, each spouse is awarded a share of the benefits if and when they are paid.

    c) **Reserved jurisdiction means that the court retains the authority to divide the pension plan at some point in the future.**

d) Cash out is just another term for the present value.

43. A; Page 22

   a) **A defined benefit retirement plan promises to pay the employee a certain amount per month at retirement time.**
   b) A defined contribution plan, such as a 401(k) plan, permits the participant to take distributions from the plan until the funds run out.
   c) A traditional IRA also permits the owner to take distributions until the money runs out.
   d) A Roth IRA also permits the owner to take tax-free distributions until the money runs out.

44. C; Page 22

   a) Present value uses the value of the future income stream and divides assets accordingly.
   b) With deferred division, each spouse is awarded a share of the benefits if and when the plan pays out.
   c) **Reserved jurisdiction should be considered a last resort, as it leaves both spouses in limbo with regard to planning for their future. The court retains authority to order distributions at some point in the future.**
   d) With the cash-out method, the assets are divided based on the present value of the plan.

45. D; Page 27

   a) A QDRO is not used to divide an IRA.
   b) A QDRO is not used to divide a Roth IRA.
   c) A QDRO is not used to divide any non-qualified benefits.
   d) **A QDRO is used to divide qualified retirement assets between the spouses. This amount can be from zero to 100%, depending on how they have divided the other assets.**

46. C; Pages 21–23

   a) A company pension has the risk of employer mismanagement of the retirement funds.
   b) A company pension has the risk of financial demise of the employer.
   c) **There is no cost of living adjustment to a 401(k) plan.**

d) A company pension does not permit participants to take any loans from the pension prior to retirement.

47. B; Page 23

    a) The total number of years worked until retirement is the denominator.

    b) **The numerator of the coverture fraction is the total number of years married while working.**

    c) The number of years single is not the numerator.

    d) The total number of years worked until the divorce is final is not the denominator.

48. A; Page 23

    a) **Some pension plans will permit the alternate payee to begin receiving benefits before the participant retires.**

    b) The retirement plan will set the age that the alternate payee can begin receiving benefits.

    c) The non-participant's retirement age is not a factor in determining when pension benefits may begin.

    d) Some companies do permit alternate payees to receive benefits before the participant retires.

49. B; Page 24

    a) This answer used an incorrect coverture fraction of 16/18. The full pension is marital property in this example.

    b) **See calculations below.**

Tim's life expectancy is 39.44 years, so he should live to be 77.44 years. Set your calculator for the beginning of the period (hit the blue button and the 7 key).

Input the following data:

    PMT   =   2,800 *(monthly payment)*

    n   =   185.28 *(number of years between age 62 and 77.44, then multiplied by 12 months)*

    i   =   .4 *(interest rate divided by 12)*

    FV =   0 *(enter 0 for the parameter you are not solving)*

Hit the PV (present value) button.

We find that the present value of the monthly payments is $366,578.46.

Now, calculate the present value as of today:

FV   =   366,578.46

n =   24 *(number of years until he is 62)*

i   =   4.8 *(interest rate)*

PMT   =   0 *(there are no payments until he retires at age 62)*

Hit the PV (present value) button.

We find that the present value is **$118,986**.

c) This the present value at age 62 using the incorrect coverture fraction of 16/18.

d) This is the present value at age 62.

50. A; Pages 23–24

a) **See calculations below.**

You begin with 17/20 or 85% of the payments to determine the marital portion of the pension payments:

$$\left(\frac{17}{20}\right) x\ 2{,}150 = \$1{,}827.50$$

Jim's life expectancy is 27.11 years, so he should live to be 79.11 years. Set your calculator for the beginning of the period (hit the blue button and the 7 key).

Input the following data:

PMT   =   1,827.50 *(monthly payment)*

n   =   169.32 *(number of years between age 65 and 79.11, then multiplied by 12 months)*

i   =   .45 *(interest rate divided by 12)*

FV =   0 *(enter 0 for the parameter you are not solving)*

Hit the PV (present value) button.

We find that the present value of the monthly payments is $216,617. This is the amount of money needed at age 65 to be able to pay Jim $1,827.50 per month for 14.11 years, which is his life expectancy.

Now, calculate the present value as of today:

FV =   216,617

n   =   13 *(number of years until he is 65)*

i   =   5.4 *(interest rate)*

PMT   =   0 *(there are no payments until he retires at age 65)*

Hit the PV (present value) button.

We find that the present value of the marital portion is **$109,336.**

b) This is the full present value; the coverture fraction for this pension is 17/20.

c) This is the present value of the marital portion at age 65.

d) This is the present value of the full pension at age 65.

51. B; Pages 25–26

a) This is the present value if you failed to use the inflation-adjusted rate.

b) **See calculations below.**

To get the inflation-adjusted interest rate, we use the following formula:

$$\left(\frac{1 + discount\ rate}{1 + inflation\ rate}\right) - 1\ x\ 100$$
$$= inflation\ adjusted\ interest$$

$$\frac{1 + .06}{1 + .03} - 1\ x\ 100 = 2.9$$

2.9 / 12 = .24 per month

Figure the present value of Mike's pension using the inflation-adjusted interest rate. Mike's life expectancy is 25.48 years; so he should live to be 79.48 years.

Again, set your calculator for the beginning of the period (hit the blue button and the 7 key).

Input the following data:

PMT   =   2,600 *(monthly payment)*

n   =   209.76 *(number of years between age 62 and 79.48, then multiplied by 12 months)*

i   =   .24272 *(interest rate divided by 12)*

FV =   0 *(enter 0 for the parameter you are not solving)*

Hit the PV (present value) button. The present value of the payments at age 62 is $426,048.50.

Between now and Mike's retirement, we use our regular interest rate because there are no payments that need to be adjusted.

Now, calculate the present value as of today:

FV =   426,048.50

n   =   8 *(number of years until he is 62)*

i   =   6 *(interest rate)*

PMT   =   0 *(there are no payments until he retires at age 62)*

Hit the PV (present value) button.

We find that the PV (present value) of Mike's inflation-protected pension is **$267,308**.

c) This is the present value of the pension at age 62 using the non-inflation adjusted rate of return.
d) This is the present value of the pension at age 62.

52. D; Page 27

a) Accrued sick pay is not a qualified plan.
b) Group term life insurance is not a qualified plan. The ex-spouse can be named as a beneficiary.
c) Disability benefits are not qualified plans.
d) **A 401(k) plan is a qualified plan and a QDRO must be used to transfer it to an alternate payee**.

53. D; Page 27

a) A QDRO also tells the administrator what happens to the assets when either party dies.
b) A QDRO also tells the administrator how the assets in the plan are to be divided.
c) A QDRO has nothing to do with IRA assets.

d) **A QDRO tells the administrator both how the assets in the plan are to be divided and what happens to the assets when either party dies.**

54. B; Page 27

a) 1974 was the year that ERISA was enacted.
b) **The REA of 1984 provides that all qualified plans subject to ERISA may segregate assets for the benefit of an alternate payee through a court order known as a Qualified Domestic Relations Order (QDRO).**
c) In 1984, the Tax Reform Act was enacted.
d) In 1997, the Tax Relief Act of 1997 was enacted.

55. A; Page 23

a) **The denominator of the coverture fraction is the total number of years worked until retirement.**
b) The numerator of the coverture fraction is total number of years married while working.
c) The number of years single while working is not the denominator.
d) The total number of years married is not the denominator.

56. D; Pages 42–43

a) There are generally three options for the home, and one is to sell the home.
b) Another option is to have one spouse buy out the other spouse's interest.
c) The third option is for both spouses to continue to own the home.
d) **Letting the home go into foreclosure is generally not a recommendation that should be made.**

57. B; Page 43

a) Wilma can transfer the home by quitclaim deed so that only Fred's name is on the title; this does not mean that she is no longer a debtor on the mortgage.
b) **Even though Wilma's name is off the deed, it remains on the mortgage. Wilma is still liable if Fred decides to stop making the payments.**
c) The mortgage company will not require Fred to refinance because Fred and Wilma are both currently responsible for the mortgage.
d) The mortgage company will not foreclose on the property as both Fred and Wilma are still responsible for the mortgage.

58. B; Pages 42–43

    a) The problem with the note payable is that it is another issue for them to deal with.

    b) **The best way to accomplish this would be to require Sally to refinance the mortgage and Marty to take another asset equal in value to the equity in the home.**

    c) Marty's credit rating could be negatively impacted if he is still on the mortgage and Sally defaults or falls behind in the mortgage payments.

    d) Marty's 401(k) is most likely all taxable. Depending on the value, Sally may be getting an asset that will not be subject to tax. If it is partially taxable upon sale then she will pay tax at the lower capital gain rates, while Marty will pay tax at ordinary rates. He will also be liable on the mortgage, so she would still need to refinance the mortgage.

59. D; Page 43

    a) Mortgage payments should be paid by both parties. They are essentially buying the asset.

    b) Major repairs should be paid by both parties since it maintains the value of the asset.

    c) Improvements should be paid by both parties since they are increasing the value of the asset.

    d) **Minor repairs should be paid by the resident spouse, since his or her use may have created the need for these repairs.**

60. B; Pages 44–46

    a) This answer deducted the mortgage value, which is not considered for taxable gain.

    b) **See calculations below.**

Sales price	$920,000
Basis	360,000
Selling expenses	35,000
Capital gain	$525,000
Kim's half of gain	$262,500
Kim's exclusion	250,000
Kim's taxable gain	**$12,500**

To calculate the taxable gain, the cost basis and the selling expenses are subtracted from the sales price. Half of this amount is the gain and then Kim's exclusion amount is subtracted from the gain to arrive at her taxable gain. The mortgage balance is irrelevant.

c) This calculation did not remove selling expense to determine taxable gain.
d) This calculation did not use Kim's available exclusion.

61. C; Pages 43–47

a) The original purchase price of the house is used to calculate the cost basis.
b) Closing costs on the purchase of the house are used to calculate the cost basis.
c) **Repairs made to the house are not considered in calculating the cost basis.**
d) Improvements made to the house are used to calculate the cost basis.

62. A; Page 45

a) **Single taxpayers can exclude $250,000 from capital gain.**
b) The mortgage balance is not relevant to calculate capital gain.
c) Married taxpayers can exclude $500,000 from capital gain.
d) Married taxpayers can exclude $500,000 from capital gain; the mortgage balance is not relevant.

63. B; Pages 45–47

a) This calculation considered the current mortgage, which is irrelevant in determining taxable gain.
b) **See calculations below.**

Sales price	$560,000
Basis	185,000
Selling expenses (5%)	28,000
Capital gain	$347,000
Lori's exclusion	250,000
Lori's taxable gain	**$97,000**

To calculate the taxable gain, the cost basis and the selling expenses are subtracted from the sales price and then Lori's exclusion amount is subtracted from the gain to arrive at her taxable gain. The mortgage balance is irrelevant.

c) This calculation did not remove selling expenses prior to determining taxable gain.

d) This calculation failed to use available exclusion amount.

64. A; Page 45

a) **The exclusion is allowed for one sale every two years.**
b) The exclusion can be used every two years, not three years.
c) The exclusion can be used every two years, not four years.
d) The exclusion can be used every two years, not five years.

65. C; Page 48

a) Even if the house is paid off there may be other expenses, including property taxes, necessary repairs, upkeep, and association fees. These may make it less cost-effective than renting or buying another property.

b) If the non-working spouse cannot afford the home long-term, then alternative housing should be seriously considered.

c) **The non-working spouse should keep the house only if it would cost more to rent or buy another suitable home. He or she also must factor into the equation the value of the home versus selling it and generating income from the proceeds.**

d) If it is more cost-effective to keep the home than to rent or buy another, then he or she may be better off keeping the home.

66. A; Pages 45–47

a) **Linda's gain is $450,000, which is the difference between the original purchase price and the sale price ($800,000 – $350,000).**

b) Linda can use John's ownership period, but not his use period, so she does not qualify for the $250,000 exclusion.

c) John did not sell the property and will not be liable for taxes on the capital gain.

d) John did not sell the property and will not be liable for taxes on the capital gain.

67. B; Pages 45–47

    a) To calculate the cost basis of a home, add the cost of improvements to the purchase price of the home.

    b) **To calculate the cost basis of a home, add the cost of improvements to the purchase price of the home.**

    c) Repairs do not increase the cost basis.

    d) Kelly does not get a step-up in basis to the date that the home was transferred to her.

68. D; Pages 69–71

    a) Judges consider the property settlement and the income generated by the property when they determine the amount of spousal support.

    b) The custodial parent may be receiving child support, but if the children are young, the parent might not be able to work full-time, which might create a need for additional spousal support.

    c) The length of the marriage is something that judges consider when determining spousal support.

    d) **The income and resources of each spouse's parents are irrelevant to calculating spousal support.**

69. D; Page 80

    a) The need of one spouse is used to determine the amount of spousal support, not child support.

    b) The ability of one spouse to pay is used to determine the amount of spousal support, not child support.

    c) The age and health of both parties is used to determine the amount of spousal support, not child support.

    d) **All states have child support guidelines, which help the courts decide the amount of child support to be paid. The courts in each state have the power to deviate from the child support guidelines and award a different amount; the state statutes set out the acceptable deviations.**

70. D; Pages 69–71

    a) Sara is more likely to receive support based on her need.

    b) Sara does not need spousal support. She has sufficient income to support herself.

c) There is no requirement that one must have minor children to be awarded spousal support.

d) **Sara is a candidate for spousal support based on her need and her husband's ability to pay.**

71. C; Page 70

a) The payor's expenses are not considered by the judge in determining the need of the recipient.

b) The judge looks at the recipient's income and the recipient's expenses.

c) **To determine the need for spousal support, the judge considers the recipient's expenses less the recipient's income.**

d) The payor is not considered when the judge is determining the need of the recipient.

72. D; Page 70

a) The recipient's expenses are not considered by the judge in determining what the payor can afford.

b) The judge considers the payor's income and expenses to determine if there is enough for the payor to live on.

c) That is how the judge determines the need of the recipient.

d) **To determine the ability to pay spousal support, the judge considers whether the payor can afford to pay what is needed and still have enough to live on.**

73. D; Page 76–77

a) The death of the recipient is one of the exceptions to the recapture rules.

b) The death of the payor is one of the exceptions to the recapture rules.

c) The remarriage of the recipient is one of the exceptions to the recapture rules.

d) **Spousal support stopping upon the cohabitation of the recipient is not an exception to the recapture rules.**

74. B; Pages 25–26

a) This calculation used the 5% interest rate—not the inflation-adjusted rate.

b) **See calculations below**.

To get the inflation-adjusted interest rate, we use the following formula:

$$\left(\frac{1 + discount\ rate}{1 + inflation\ rate}\right) - 1\ x\ 100$$

$$= inflation\ adjusted\ interest$$

$$\frac{1 + .05}{1 + .03} - 1\ x\ 100 = 1.94175$$

Figure the present value using the inflation-adjusted interest rate. Tony's life expectancy is 33.11 years; so he should live to be 78.11 years. Again, set your calculator for the beginning of the period (hit the blue button and the 7 key).

Input the following data:

PMT = 2,850 *(monthly payment)*

n = 157.32 *(number of years between age 65 and 78.11, then multiplied by 12 months)*

i = .16181 *(interest rate divided by 12)*

FV = 0 *(enter 0 for the parameter you are not solving)*

Hit the PV (present value) button.

The present value of the payments at age 65 is $395,290.

Between now and Tony's retirement, we use our regular interest rate because there are no payments that need to be adjusted.

Now, calculate the Present Value as of today:

FV = 395,290

n = 20 *(number of years until he is 65)*

i = 5 *(interest rate)*

PMT = 0 *(there are no payments until he retires at age 65)*

Hit the PV (present value) button.

We find that the present value of Tony's inflation-protected pension is **$148,981**.

c) This calculation used 5% interest instead of the inflation-adjusted figure to find the present value of the plan at age 65.

d) This calculation used the inflation-adjusted figure, but found the present value of the plan at age 65—not the current present value of the plan.

75. C; Page 71

    a) Rehabilitative maintenance does not have anything to do with a disability.

    b) Rehabilitative maintenance does not have anything to do with a child's disability.

    c) **The purpose of rehabilitative maintenance is to provide temporary financial help until the recipient is able to earn enough to be self-sufficient.**

    d) Rehabilitative maintenance is not permanent financial assistance.

76. C; Pages 73–74

    a) Payments for property owned by the payor do not qualify as support.

    b) Support for children does not count as spousal support.

    c) **Support payments to the ex-spouse pursuant to a court order qualify as spousal support.**

    d) Payments to the ex-spouse that are outside of the judgment do not count as support.

77. C; Page 75

    a) Mike cannot deduct $800 as spousal support because performing a service does not qualify as spousal support.

    b) Mike has not complied with the court order because he cannot work in lieu of paying support.

    c) **Mike cannot substitute a service for a payment to his ex-spouse pursuant to a court order, so he cannot deduct $800 as spousal support.**

    d) It does not count as support because it is not in cash or its equivalent.

78. C; Page 75

    a) Since the payment is not pursuant to a court order, it is not deductible.

    b) George cannot deduct the extra support, since it is not pursuant to a court order.

    c) **George cannot deduct the extra $500 as spousal support because it was not a payment to his ex-spouse pursuant to a court order.**

    d) George cannot deduct the extra $500 even if Jane were to claim it as income.

79. D; Page 76

    a) Their filing status is determined based on their marital status as of December 31 of the year they are filing. Since Mary's divorce was final on December 18, 2014, she may not file a joint return.

    b) Mary can file as single, but she could also file as head of household.

    c) Mary can file as head of household, but she could also file as single.

    d) **Mary can file as either single or head of household. If Mary has a dependent child who lives in her household, and if she provides more than half of the child's support, then she would qualify as head of household.**

80. A; Pages 76–77

    a) **Pursuant to IRC §71(f)(1)(B), if payments drop by more than $15,000 in the first three years, recapture rules are triggered.**

    b) This is a permissible drop in spousal support.

    c) Any decline in payments after year three does not trigger recapture rules.

    d) This is not recapture. However, because it is violating the multiple-reduction rule, it will trigger a re-characterization of the deductible spousal support to nondeductible child support from the beginning of the payments.

81. C; Pages 76–77

    a) The death of either spouse is an exception to the recapture rules.

    b) If spousal support is based on a percentage of income, then recapture does not apply.

    c) **A decline in spousal support of $20,000 in year three would trigger recapture.**

    d) A decline in spousal support in year four does not trigger recapture.

82. A; Page 81

    a) **Only when the amount of child support is dependent on spousal support does this apply.**

    b) It is an inverse relationship; in this case, both decrease.

    c) It is an inverse relationship; in this case, both increase.

    d) There is an inverse relationship in some states.

83. A; Page 82

    a) **Since circumstances can change after the divorce is final, child support is always modifiable.**

    b) Spousal support is modifiable, unless the parties have agreed in the decree that it is not modifiable.

    c) Property division is not modifiable.

    d) The only way to modify a divorce is to get remarried.

84. C; Page 83

    a) The tax exemption for children can also be transferred for more than one year.

    b) The tax exemption for children can also be transferred for only one year.

    c) **The tax exemption can be transferred to the non-custodial parent for one or more years using a written waiver or IRS Form 8332. Once the custodial parent has executed the waiver, the non-custodial parent must attach the form to his or her income tax return. If the waiver is for more than one year, a copy of the form must be attached to the non-custodial parent's return each year.**

    d) The tax exemption for children can be transferred.

85. B; Pages 83–84

    a) This answer says "one year." The correct duration is six months.

    b) **Spousal support payments are re-characterized as child support when spousal support is reduced not more than six months before or after the date on which the child reaches age 18, 21, or the age of majority in their state.**

    c) Spousal support can be re-characterized as child support—not vice-versa. The rule is also six months, not one year.

    d) Spousal support can be re-characterized as child support—not vice-versa.

86. B; Page 84

    a) The rule does not apply to a reduction in child support payments.

    b) **Spousal support payments are re-characterized as child support when the spousal support payments are to be reduced on two or more occasions that occur not more than one year before or after each child reaches a certain age; if that happens, it is presumed that the amount of the reduction is child support. The age at which the reduction occurs** must be between 18 and 24, inclusive, and must be the same for each of the children.

c) This rule does not apply to a reduction in child support payments.

d) This rule applies when there is more than one child – not when there are two reductions for one child.

87. B; Pages 86–87

a) Margaret could take benefits based on half of Louis' benefit. However, this is not the highest benefit she could receive.

b) **Margaret can only take benefits from one account, so she must choose which account she will take benefits from: $820 from her own account, $625 from Louis's account, or $540 from Harold's account. Obviously, she should take benefits from her own account, which would pay her $820 per month.**

c) If Harold were deceased, she would be able to get his full benefit.

d) If Louis were deceased, she would be able to get his full benefit.

88. D; Page 87

a) There is no limit on the number of wives who may collect Social Security benefits.

b) There is no limit on the number of wives who may collect Social Security benefits.

c) There is no limit on the number of wives who may collect Social Security benefits.

d) **There is no limit on the number of wives who can collect Social Security benefits. As long as he is married to each one for ten years or longer, they each get half of his Social Security benefit.**

89. A; Pages 87–88

a) **Sally does not qualify for widow's benefits because has not reached the age of 60.**

b) Sally must wait until she is 62 to collect retirement benefits on her spouse's account.

c) Sally cannot collect on her own account until she is 62.

d) Sally will be able to collect widow's benefits at age 60.

90. D; Page 90

    a) COBRA coverage can be provided for longer than 12 months.

    b) Eighteen months is the coverage an employee gets if he or she is no longer employed by the employer.

    c) An employee's ex-spouse may be eligible for COBRA insurance coverage for 36 months after the divorce.

    d) **Since there are 20 or more employees, she is eligible for COBRA for 36 months.**

91. B; Page 90

    a) The law was not passed in 1980.

    b) **The Consolidated Omnibus Budget Reconciliation Act (COBRA) law was passed in 1986.**

    c) The law was not passed in 1992.

    d) The law was not passed in 2000.

92. D; Page 91

    a) Life insurance is required to cover spousal and child support only if the judge orders it.

    b) Life insurance can be required for spousal support if the judge orders it, not just if the spouse requests it.

    c) Life insurance can be required for child support if the judge orders it, but also can be required to cover spousal support.

    d) **Life insurance is only required if the judge orders it. It can be used to protect both child support and spousal support payments.**

93. A; Page 92

    a) **Insurance should be obtained as soon as the parties have an idea it is required. If the spouse cannot get insurance (for health reasons, etc.), the settlement can be changed to make up for the lack of insurance.**

    b) This is not enough time to have an insurance policy in effect. If something were to happen before there was a policy in place, it could bring major financial harm.

    c) This is too late to apply for insurance.

    d) An existing policy can be used, but a new policy can be purchased and may make more sense.

94. A; Page 96

    a) **Chapter 7 bankruptcy allows an individual to liquidate all of the assets and use the proceeds to pay off debts, erasing the debts that cannot be paid in full.**

    b) Chapter 11 bankruptcy is for businesses.

    c) Chapter 12 bankruptcy is for farmers and fisherman.

    d) Chapter 13 bankruptcy allows an individual to pay off debts over three years. Some of the unsecured debts may be discharged.

95. D; Page 93

    a) If one of them stops making payments on one of the credit cards, the other would be responsible for the payments.

    b) If Alex stops making payments, Kim would be responsible for the payments and he would end up with an extra $5,000. She would be able to collect through the courts, but it would cost more money and time.

    c) If Kim stops making payments, Alex would be responsible for the payments and she would end up with an extra $5,000. He would also be able to collect through the courts, but it would cost more money and time.

    d) **The best option is for them to pay off the credit cards. That way, each will not be able to affect the other's credit post-divorce.**

96. D; Page 93

    a) The divorce decree does not terminate Claire's liability to the credit card company.

    b) They are both liable; it is irrelevant who incurred the debt.

    c) Matt is still liable for this debt.

    d) **This is a joint debt and they will both be liable to the credit card company. However, Matt will be the one that must make the payments according to the judgment.**

97. A; Page 97

    a) **Property settlement notes, especially unsecured notes, are almost always discharged in bankruptcy.**

    b) Child support in arrears cannot be discharged in bankruptcy.

    c) Spousal support in arrears cannot be discharged in bankruptcy.

    d) Student loans cannot be discharged in bankruptcy.

98. D; Page 91

  a) If Madge owns the policy, she will know that the insurance premiums have been paid and that she is still the beneficiary.

  b) If Madge owns the policy, she will know that the insurance premiums have been paid and that she is still the beneficiary.

  c) Being an irrevocable beneficiary for a policy that Gerald owns also offers some protection for Madge.

  d) **The policy at work can be terminated or the beneficiary can be changed. This offers the least protection.**

99. C; Pages 13–14

  a) A CDFA professional should also consider the depreciating assets.

  b) A CDFA professional should also consider the appreciating assets.

  c) **Both appreciating assets and depreciating assets should be considered.**

  d) A CDFA professional should consider both.

100. B; Page 30

  a) The PBGC does not calculate the present value of pensions.

  b) **The Pension Benefit Guaranty Corporation (PBGC), which is a federal corporation, announces the monthly interest rates for the following month. The rate used to calculate the present value of pension plans is based on average annuity rates.**

  c) The PBGC does not draft QDROs.

  d) The PBGC does not require tax withholdings from IRAs.

SAMPLE TAX RATES

(Tax rates will be provided on exams. Rates listed are for testing purposes only. Current rates may vary.)

A. SCHEDULE X: Single Filers

Taxable Income			Tax
$0	to	$8,500	10% of taxable income
8,501	to	34,500	$850 plus 15% of excess over $8,500
34,501	to	83,600	$4,750 plus 25% of excess over $34,500
83,601	to	174,400	$17,025 plus 28% of excess over $83,600
174,401	to	379,150	$42,449 plus 33% of excess over $174,400
379,151	and up		$110,016.50 plus 35% of excess over $379,15

B. SCHEDULE Z: Head of Household

Taxable Income			Tax
$0	to	$12,150	10% of taxable income
12,151	to	46,250	$1,215 plus 15% of excess over $12,150
46,251	to	119,400	$6,330 plus 25% of excess over $46,250
119,401	to	193,350	$24,617.50 plus 28% of excess over $119,400
193,351	to	379,150	$45,323.50 plus 33% of excess over $193,350
379,151	and up		$106,637.50 plus 35% of excess over $379,15

C. SCHEDULE Y-1: Married Filing Jointly and Surviving Spouse

Taxable Income			Tax
$0	to	$17,000	10% of taxable income
17,001	to	69,000	$1,700 plus 15% of excess over $17,000
69,001	to	139,350	$9,500 plus 25% of excess over $69,000
139,351	to	212,300	$27,087.50 plus 28% of excess over $139,350
212,301	to	379,150	$47,513.50 plus 33% of excess over $212,300
379,151	and up		102,574 plus 35% of excess over $379,150

D. SCHEDULE Y-2: Married Filing Separately

Taxable Income			Tax
$0	to	$8,500	10% of taxable income
8,501	to	34,500	$850 plus 15% of excess over $8,500
34,500	to	69,675	$4,750 plus 25% of excess over $34,500
69,676	to	106,150	$13,543.75 plus 28% of excess over $69,675
106,151	to	189,575	$23,756.75 plus 33% of excess over $106,150
189,576	and up		$51,287 plus 35% of excess over $189,575

STANDARD DEDUCTIONS

Single Filers: $5,800   Married filing jointly: $11,600

Head of Household: $8,500   Married filing separately: $5,800

PERSONAL EXEMPTION

The personal exemption is $3,700 per person

SOCIAL SECURITY DEDUCTIONS

FICA   4.2% on the first $106,800 of income

Medicare   1.45% on all income (no limit)

SAMPLE LIFE EXPECTANCY

Completed Age	Life Expectancy Male	Female
0	75.10	80.21
1	74.66	79.70
2	73.69	78.73
3	72.72	77.75
4	71.74	76.77
5	70.75	75.78
6	69.76	74.79
7	68.77	73.80
8	67.79	72.81
9	66.79	71.82
10	65.80	70.82
11	64.81	69.83
12	63.81	68.84
13	62.82	67.85
14	61.84	66.86
15	60.86	65.87
16	59.90	64.89
17	58.94	63.91
18	58.00	62.93
19	57.60	61.96
20	56.13	60.99
21	55.20	60.01
22	54.28	59.04
23	53.37	58.07
24	52.45	57.10
25	51.53	56.13
26	50.61	55.16
27	49.68	54.19
28	48.75	53.22
29	47.82	52.25
30	46.89	51.28
31	45.96	50.32
32	45.02	49.35
33	44.09	48.39
34	43.16	47.42
35	42.23	46.46
36	41.30	45.50
37	40.37	44.55
38	39.44	43.59
39	38.52	42.65
40	37.61	41.70
41	36.69	40.76
42	35.79	39.82
43	34.89	38.89
44	34.00	37.96
45	33.11	37.04
46	32.23	35.8
47	31.35	35.21
48	30.49	34.30
49	29.63	33.39
50	28.78	32.49

Completed Age	Life Expectancy Male	Female
51	27.94	31.60
52	27.11	30.71
53	26.29	29.83
54	25.48	28.94
55	24.66	28.07
56	23.86	27.20
57	23.06	26.33
58	22.26	25.47
59	21.48	24.62
60	20.70	23.78
61	19.94	22.95
62	19.19	22.13
63	18.45	21.32
64	17.72	20.52
65	17.00	19.72
66	16.28	18.94
67	15.58	18.19
68	14.89	17.40
69	14.22	16.64
70	13.55	15.90
71	12.91	15.18
72	12.27	14.47
73	11.65	13.78
74	11.05	13.10
75	10.46	12.43
76	9.89	11.78
77	9.34	11.14
78	8.80	10.52
79	8.29	9.92
80	7.78	9.33
81	7.30	8.76
82	6.84	8.21
83	6.39	7.68
84	5.97	7.17
85	5.56	6.68
86	5.18	6.22
87	4.81	5.78
88	4.46	5.37
89	4.14	4.98
90	3.84	4.62
91	3.56	4.28
92	3.30	3.98
93	3.07	3.69
94	2.86	3.44
95	2.67	3.20
96	2.51	3.00
97	2.36	2.81
98	2.24	2.65
99	2.12	2.49
100	2.01	2.35
101	1.90	2.20

GLOSSARY

Appraisal: Procedure for determining the fair market value of an asset when it is to be sold or divided as part of the divorce process.

Arbitration: Submitting a disputed matter for decision to a person who is not a judge. The decision of an arbitrator is usually binding and final. Arbitration varies greatly from mediation.

Arrearages: The difference between the amount of spousal or child support paid, if any, and the amount required under court order.

Assets: Cash, property, investments, goodwill, and other items of value (as defined by state law) that appear on a balance sheet indicating the net worth of an individual or a business.

Asset Inventory: Collection of financial data that includes information on assets and liabilities. Key documents used are the Financial Affidavit and Asset/Liability Comparison worksheet.

Bankruptcy: See Chapter 7 Bankruptcy and Chapter 13 Bankruptcy.

Best Interest of the Child: A discretionary legal standard used by judges when making decisions about custody, visitation, and support for a child when the parents are divorcing.

Bunching Deductions: Tax strategy that involves "bunching" itemized deductions so that they are high in one year and low the following year. The standard deduction can be used on the alternate year.

Career Asset: Assets tied to one's career (health insurance, stock options, retirement plans, etc.)

Certified Business Appraiser (CBA): An individual who is certified in business valuations.

Change of Venue: A change of judges or geographical location, requested by a party to the action who feels that the change is justified by state law.

Chapter 7 Bankruptcy: Type of bankruptcy filing that allows you to liquidate all of your assets and use the proceeds to pay off your debts, erasing your debts that cannot be paid off in full. All unsecured debts are forgiven and all assets over statutory minimum protected amounts are forfeited.

Chapter 13 Bankruptcy: Type of bankruptcy filing that allows you to develop a pay-off plan over a three-year period. Some of the debts may be discharged.

Childcare Credit: (dependency exemption) a nonrefundable childcare tax credit available to the custodial parent who pays for child or dependent care expenses so that they can be gainfully employed.

Child Contingency Rule: States that if any amount of spousal support specified in the divorce decree is reduced: (a) upon the happening of any contingency related to the child; or (b) at a time that can be clearly associated with a contingency related to the child, then the amount of the reduction will be treated as child support, rather than spousal support. These payments will be considered child support when the payments begin. (IRS Code Section 71(c)(2))

Child Support: The amount of money paid by a non-custodial parent to the custodial parent for a child's day-to-day expenses and other special needs. Each state is required by Congress to have written child support guidelines and enforcement procedures.

Child Support Guidelines: A series of mathematical formulas used to calculate the amount of child support to be paid in some cases. Congress has mandated that states adopt child support guidelines and support enforcement procedures.

COBRA: Consolidated Omnibus Budget Reconciliation Act (COBRA) law passed in 1986. It allows an ex-spouse to continue to receive health insurance coverage from his/her former spouse's employer if the employer has at least 20 employees, for up to three years after the divorce. Premiums for this coverage are typically higher than when they were covered under the employer's plan. It should be noted that the normal COBRA provision states that if an employee leaves or is fired from a job, he or she can get health insurance from that company for 18 months. However, in the case of a divorce it is extended to three years or 36 months.

Collaborative Divorce: A team approach to divorce in which divorcing couples obtain professional help from specialists in the legal, financial, and mental health fields; when needed, additional professionals (including child/parenting experts) may be called in to help the couple settle their case.

Collaborative Law: Collaborative Law is a new dispute resolution model in which each party retains their own attorney who has gone through specialized "Collaborative Law" training. The lawyer's only job is to help settle the dispute. All parties agree to work together respectfully, honestly, and in good faith to try to find "win-win" solutions to the legitimate needs of both parties. No one may go to court, or even threaten to do so. If that should occur, the Collaborative Law process terminates and both lawyers are disqualified from any further involvement in the case.

Collusion: An agreement between two or more persons where one of the parties brings false charges against the other. In a divorce case, the husband and wife may agree to use adultery as a ground in order to obtain divorce more quickly, knowing full well that adultery was not committed. Collusion is illegal.

Common Law Marriage: A judicially recognized marriage in some states, usually based on cohabitation where no formal marriage ceremony has taken place. See page 35 for more details.

Community Property: In community property states, any property not deemed "separate" (i.e., owned before the marriage or obtained by gift or inheritance) is "community" property and will likely be subject to a 50/50 division. Any property acquired in a community property state retains its community property status no matter where the couple moves. There are currently eight states that have adopted community property laws: Arizona, California, Idaho, Louisiana, Nevada, New Mexico, Texas, and Washington. Alaska has an optional community property act (AS 34.77.090), and Wisconsin is essentially a community property state, but there are exceptions to the typical community property rules. Most other states follow the rule of "equitable distribution" of property.

Complainant: The one who files the suit; same as plaintiff.

Complaint: This is a legal document filed by the plaintiff to start the divorce process. It states that the marriage has ended and lists the grounds and claims for the divorce. In some states it is also known as a petition.

Condonation: The act of forgiving one's spouse who has committed an act of wrongdoing that would constitute grounds for divorce. Condonation generally is proven by living and cohabitating with the spouse after learning that the wrongdoing was committed. It is often used as a defense to a divorce.

Jim

Contempt of Court: The willful failure to comply with a court order, judgment, or decree by a party to the actions. Contempt of Court may be punishable by fine or imprisonment.

Contested Divorce: Any case where the judge must decide one or more issues that are not agreed to by the parties. All cases are considered contested until all issues have been agreed to.

DAVE

Corroborative Witness: A person who testifies for one of the parties and backs up their story.

Cost Basis: The original value of an asset for tax purposes.

Court Order: A written instruction from the court carrying the weight of law. Orders must be in writing. Anyone who knowingly violates a court order can be held in contempt of court.

Coverture Fraction: Used to separate the portion of the benefits in a pension plan earned during marriage from the portion earned outside of the marriage. Under this approach, the alternate payee's share of the benefit is based on the participant's benefit at the participant's date of retirement (when it is highest). Once the participant's final benefit is calculated, the marital portion is determined by multiplying the accrued benefit by a coverture fraction: the number of years married while earning the pension divided by the total number of years of service under the plan until retirement. The alternate payee would then be entitled to half of the marital portion of the ultimate pension.

Credit: The measure of trustworthiness of repayment of a loan based on income, past credit history, assets, and liabilities. It should be noted that after the divorce the former spouses' past credit history might affect the ex-spouse.

Cross Examination: The questioning of a witness presented by the opposing party on trial or at a deposition. The purpose is to test the truth of that testimony.

Curriculum Vitae: A resume that is prepared by an expert witness to show their qualifications in their area of expertise.

Custodial Parent: The parent with whom the child(ren) live the majority of the time. A distinction should be made between a Legal Guardian (who has the ability to make legal decisions on behalf of the child) and the Custodial Parent: Technically, a Legal Guardian may have no custody rights at all.

Custody: Usually refers to the parent's right to (1) have a child live with that parent and (2) make decisions concerning the child. Exact meaning varies greatly in different states. The court awards custody to one parent, which is called Sole Custody, or grants Joint Custody, allowing both parents, the right to physical care, control, or direct physical supervision of the children.

Debt: Services, money, or goods owed by one party to another.

Decree: The final ruling of the judge on an action for divorce, legal separation, or annulment. Decree has the same meaning as judgment.

Decree Nisi / Rule Nisi: An order by the court stating that a conditional divorce will become absolute by a certain date, unless a party contests the order.

Default: A party's failure to answer a complaint, motion, or petition.

Defendant: The partner in a marriage against whom a divorce complaint is filed. Defendant has the same meaning as respondent.

Deferred Division or Future Share Method: One of three methods that can be used to divide pension benefits. No present value is determined. Each spouse is awarded a share of the benefits if and when they are paid.

Deposition: The testimony of a witness taken out of court under oath and reduced to writing. Discovery depositions are the most common and are taken for the purpose of discovering the facts upon which a party's claim is based or discovering the substance of a witness's testimony prior to trial. The deposition may be used to discredit a witness if he changes his testimony.

Defined Benefit Plan: Type of employer-sponsored pension plan that promises to pay the employee a certain amount per month at retirement time. It does not have a cash value today.

Direct Examination: The initial questioning of a witness by the attorney who called him or her to the stand.

Discovery: Procedures followed by attorneys in order to determine the nature, scope, and credibility of the opposing party's claim. Discovery procedures include depositions, written interrogatories, and notices to produce documentation relating to issues relevant to the case.

Dismissal: Occurs when a party voluntarily drops the case (in some states) or when a judge finds that a case totally lacks merit.

Dissolution of Marriage: The legal process of ending a marriage. In most states, the legal term for divorce.

Division of Assets: This is dependent upon the statutes governing property division in the state where the divorcing couple resides. States have adopted two property division statutes: community property and equitable distribution.

Divorce: The legal proceeding by which a marriage is legally terminated. It may be contested (where one party denies the allegation or wants to keep the marriage in place) or uncontested.

Divorce Expenses: Costs incurred during the divorce process that can include court filing fees, appraisals, mediation fees, legal fees, accounting, financial planning, counseling, QDRO preparation, and tax preparation.

Domestic Violence: The physical abuse of one family member by another.

Double Dipping: When one spouse gets paid twice from the same asset.

Earned Income Tax Credit: (IRC §32) A custodial parent is entitled to an increased tax income credit if he or she has a qualifying child that meets IRS requirements. Also see Section 32 below.

Emancipation: The point at which a minor child comes of age. Children are emancipated in most states upon reaching the age of 18, 19, or 21, or upon marriage, full-time employment, graduation from high school, or entering the armed services. Emancipation is the point where parents have no further legal or financial obligations for a child's support.

Employee Retirement Income Security Act of 1974 (ERISA): A federal law that sets minimum standards for pension plans in private industry. ERISA does not require any employer to establish a pension plan – it only requires that those who establish plans must meet certain minimum standards. The law generally does not specify how much money a participant must be paid as a benefit. ERISA requires plans to regularly provide participants with information about the plan including information about plan features and funding; sets minimum standards for participation, vesting, benefit accrual, and funding; requires accountability of plan fiduciaries; and gives participants the right to sue for benefits and breaches of fiduciary duty. ERISA also guarantees payment of certain benefits through the Pension Benefit Guaranty Corporation, a federally chartered corporation, if a defined plan is terminated.

Equitable: Means fair; does not necessarily mean equal.

Equitable Division of Property: Method of dividing property based on a number of considerations (such as length of marriage, differences in age, wealth, earning potential, and health of partners involved) to achieve an equitable and fair distribution—not necessarily an equal one. Eight of the western states use a different method of division called Community Property.

Evidence: Proof presented at a hearing, including testimony, documents, or objects.

Exhibits: Tangible things presented at trial as evidence.

Expert Witness: In court proceedings, the expert witness is the professional whose testimony helps a judge reach a decision.

File/Filing: To place a document in the official custody of some public official. Every case brought to court must be filed with the court clerk in order for the court to take action upon the case. A case is filed when a party (plaintiff) writes a written complaint and brings it to the clerk, who files it. The plaintiff must also serve the opposing party with a copy of the complaint.

Financial Affidavit: Key document used to collect financial data; in some states, it may be known as a "Financial Statement" and may use a standard form. This document becomes part of the record of documents that are filed with the court. Included in the Financial Affidavit are all income and deductions from income, all living expenses, all assets, and all liabilities.

Foundation: The evidence that must be presented before asking certain questions or offering documentary evidence in trial. If a piece of evidence lacks foundation (proof, facts to back it up) it will not be admitted or considered as evidence in the court case.

Garnishing: The act by which support money is obtained from the non-paying spouse's employer, who draws that amount from his/her employee's paycheck.

General Agreement on Tariffs and Trade (GATT) Rate: Interest rate based on 30 year Treasury bond interest rate and is used as a benchmark for calculations of lump sum distribution from defined benefit plans.

Goodwill: The value of a business beyond its sales revenue, inventory, and other tangible assets: including prestige, name recognition, and customer loyalty.

Grounds for Divorce: Reasons for seeking a divorce, such as incompatibility, mental cruelty, physical abuse, or adultery. While some states allow fault grounds for divorce, all states have some form of no-fault divorce.

Guardian-ad-Litem: A person appointed by a judge to prosecute or defend a case for a person legally unable to do so, such as a minor child.

Hearing: Any proceeding before a judicial officer.

Hearsay: Hearsay is an out-of-court statement offered to prove the truth of the matter asserted. Generally speaking, hearsay cannot be used at trial, but there are exceptions that permit it to be admitted to court.

Incompatibility: The inability of persons to get along; a ground for divorce.

Innocent Spouse Rule (IRC §6015): Provides tax liability relief for a spouse who signs a joint tax return and has no knowledge of the understatement of tax. In order to qualify, the following requirements must be met:
- That a joint return was filed.

- There was an understatement of tax attributable to erroneous items from one spouse filing the joint return.

- That in signing the return, the innocent spouse did not know, and had no reason to know, and there was an understatement of tax.

- That taking into account all of the facts and circumstances, it would be inequitable to hold the innocent spouse liable for the deficiency in tax.

- The innocent spouse elects the benefits no later than two years after the date the IRS has begun collection activities with respect to the individual making the election.

Interest-Based Bargaining: A method of negotiation used in mediation. It starts with each party educating the other party about their interests. Ideally, the parties will work together until they find solutions that allow both parties to meet their needs.

Interrogatories: A series of written questions served upon the opposing party in order to discover certain facts regarding the disputed issues in a matrimonial proceeding.

Joint Custody: The children live with the residential custodian and visit with the non-residential parent. Both parents have an equal say in major decisions affecting the children and decisions can only be made with notice and consent. *See also Sole Custody*.

Joint Property: Property held in the name of more than one person.

Judgment: The order of the court on a disputed issue; same as decree.

Jurisdiction: The power of the court to rule upon issues relating to the parties, their children, or their property.

Legal Separation: Court ruling on division of property, spousal support, and responsibility to children when a couple wishes to separate but not divorce. A legal separation is most often desired for religious or medical reasons. A decree of legal separation does not dissolve the marriage and does not allow the parties to remarry. Texas does not recognize legal separation.

Limited Divorce: Establishes certain legal responsibilities while the parties are separated but does not end the marriage. Also referred to as legal separation.

Lis Pendens: A piece of property cannot be transferred during a pending lawsuit that may change the disposition of it once a notice has been filed in the public record.

Litigation: The process by which a civil case settles parties' rights.

Maintenance: Same as spousal support and alimony.

Marital Property: Accumulated income and property acquired by the spouses during the marriage subject to equitable division by the court. States will vary on their precise definition of what is to be included in marital property, sometimes excepting property acquired by gift or inheritance. See also "Community Property" and "Equitable Division of Property."

Mediation: A non-adversarial process in which a husband and wife are assisted in reaching their own terms of divorce by a neutral third party trained in divorce matters. The mediator has no power to make or enforce decisions. Mediation differs greatly from Arbitration.

Modification: A change in the judgment based on a change in circumstances.

Motion: An application or request to the court for an order. May be written or verbal.

Multiple Reduction Rule: Second provision in the Child Contingency rule when there is more than one child. If spousal support payments are reduced on two or more occasions, which occur not more than one year before or after each child reaches a certain age, then it is presumed that the amount of the reduction is child support. The age at which the reduction occurs must be between 18 and 24 inclusive and must be the same for each of the children.

No Fault Divorce: A marriage dissolution system whereby divorce is granted without the necessity of proving one of the parties guilty of marital misconduct.

Non-Custodial Parent: The parent with whom the children do not live the majority of the time.

Nuptial: Pertaining to marriage.

Order: A ruling by the court.

Paralegal: A legal assistant to an attorney, usually certified by the state, who is trained in legal research.

Pendente Lite Support: A temporary order of the Court that provides support until the divorce is finalized. See also temporary order.

Pension Benefit Guaranty Corporation (PBGC): A federal corporation created by the government that announces monthly interest rates (for the following month) that are used to calculate the present value of pension plans. This rate is based on average annuity rates.

Perjury: The act of lying while under oath.

Personal Exemption: A tax deduction for individual taxpayer and any qualifying dependents they support.

Petition: A written application for particular relief from the court. In some jurisdictions complaint for divorce is entitled "petition for dissolution."

Petitioner: The person who filed the Petition or Complaint. Also referred to as the Plaintiff.

Physical Custody: The parent with whom the children will primarily reside. See "Custodial Parent."

Plaintiff: The spouse who initiates the legal divorce process by filing a complaint or petition stating that the marriage is over and listing the grounds and claims against the other spouse. Plaintiff is the same as Petitioner.

Positional Bargaining: Positional bargaining starts with the solution. One party proposes a solution and the other party makes an offer. Counteroffers are made until a resolution is found that works for both parties.

Precedent: Decisions found in other pre-existing cases which factor into the case at hand.

Prenuptial Agreement: Prior to a marriage, partners contractually agree how assets and liabilities will be divided in the event of a divorce. Prenuptial agreements are usually upheld, absent fraud, coercion, duress, or severe misrepresentation.

Present Value or Cash-Out Method: One of three methods that can be used to divide pension benefits. The non-employee spouse is paid a lump-sum settlement from the pension or receives a marital asset of equal value to the non-employee spouse's interest in the pension.

Primary Caregiver: A factor in consideration of who should be the custodial parent, the person who usually takes care of the children.

Privilege: The right of a spouse to make admissions to an attorney, clergyman, psychiatrist, or others as designated by state law that are not later admissible as evidence.

Property Settlement Note: A note from the payor to the payee for an agreed-upon length of time with a reasonable interest rate. Can be collateralized.

Pro Se Divorce: A divorce wherein the divorcing partners represent themselves in court (with or without a mutually agreeable separation agreement) without the assistance of attorneys. Pro Se is Latin for Proper Person.

Qualified Domestic Relations Order (QDRO): A court ruling earmarking a portion of a person's retirement or pension fund payments to be paid to his/her ex-spouse as part of a division of marital assets. The fund administrator makes payments directly to the non-employee ex-spouse at the time of the divorce or at the time the employee's retirement payments are to begin.

Qualified Principal Residence Indebtedness: Any debt incurred in acquiring, constructing, or substantially improving a principal residence and which is secured by the principal residence. It also includes any debt secured by the principal residence resulting from the refinancing of debt incurred to acquire, construct, or substantially improve the principal residence but only to the extent the amount of debt does not exceed the amount refinanced debt.

Quid Pro Quo: The giving of one valuable thing for another.

Rebuttal: The introduction of evidence at a trial that is in response to new material raised by the defendant at an earlier stage of the trial.

Recapture: Deductions taken in a previous year's income.

Recapture Rule: A rule that comes into effect if spousal support payments decrease annually in excess of $15,000 during the first three calendar years.

Reconciliation: When parties decide to get back together. They may sign a reconciliation agreement, which is enforceable by the court.

Rehabilitative Maintenance: Temporary financial support given to an ex-spouse until they are able to earn a sufficient amount to support themselves.

Reserved Jurisdiction: One of three methods that can be used to divide pension benefits. In this instance, the court retains authority to order distributions from a pension plan at some point in the future.

Respondent (Defendant): The party defending against a divorce petition (complaint).

Restraining Order: A court order prohibiting a party from certain activities. Issued in response to a motion. Restraining orders are often issued to protect against domestic violence or to protect marital assets. In many states, violating a "domestic restraining order" is a criminal offense.

Retirement Equity Act of 1984 (REA): This Act amended ERISA to introduce mandatory spousal rights in pension plans so the choice of the form of benefit received from a pension plan was no longer solely the participant's choice.

Retainer: Money paid by the client to the lawyer or expert witness to obtain a commitment from the lawyer or expert witness to handle the client's case. A retainer can be a deposit against which the lawyer or expert witness charges fees as they are earned.

Revenue Act of 1942: Requires certain spousal support payments to be included in the recipient spouse's income and permitted the payor spouse to deduct these payments as an itemized deduction.

Rules of Evidence: The rules that govern the method of presentation and admissibility of oral and documentary evidence at court hearings or depositions.

Schedule A: Itemized Deductions.
Schedule B: Interest and Ordinary Dividends.

Schedule C: Profit or Loss from Business.

Schedule D: Capital Gains and Losses.

Schedule E: Supplemental Income and Loss.

Section 32 EITC IRC: This section of the IRS Code states that the custodial parent is entitled to increased earned tax income credit if he or she has a qualifying child and meets the requirements. See also "Earned Income Tax Credit."

Section 71 Payments: This section of the IRS Code states that alimony and separate maintenance payments are generally taxable to the recipient and deductible from gross income by the payor. These payments can be treated as alimony for tax purposes if:

- The payment is made in cash, check, or money order.
- There must be a written court order or separation agreement.
- The couple may not agree that the payments are not to receive alimony tax treatment.
- They may not be residing in the same household.
- They may not file a joint tax return.
- No portion of the payment may be considered child support.

Additionally, Section 71 requires that if the payor of alimony wants to deduct alimony payments over $15,000 per year, payments must last for at least three years. If this requirement is not met, payments are subject to recapture rules.

Section 72: This section of the IRS Code allows the alternate payee to receive money from a qualified plan, pursuant to a QDRO, without having to pay a 10% tax penalty. The distribution would still be subject to ordinary income tax.

Section 1041: This section of the IRS Code states that any transfer of property between spouses during marriage (or former spouses if it is incident to divorce) is tax free. No gain or loss is recognized and for income tax purposes, the transferee's basis and holding period in the property is the adjusted basis and holding period of the transferor. An assignment of an annuity contract is non-taxable for both the transferor spouse and the transferee spouse under this section.

Section 6015: See the "Innocent Spouse" rule.

Section 7703(b): This section of the IRS Code states that a spouse is considered abandoned when all of the following conditions are met:

- The abandoned spouse pays more than half the cost of maintaining his/her household for the taxable year.

- The individual files a separate tax return.

- The individual's household is the principal home of a dependent child for more than six months of the tax year and the individual is entitled to claim the dependency exemption (even if no claim is made).

- The individual lives in a residence separate from his /her spouse for the last six months of the tax year.

Secured Debt: A loan secured by collateral to reduce the risk associated with lending. Mortgages and auto loans are examples of secured debt.

Separate Property: Generally considered any property owned before marriage (earned or acquired by gift or inheritance), acquired during the marriage by one partner using only that partner's separate property, or earned after a formalized agreement. This definition will vary from state to state.

Separation: The court grants a legal separation. It grants the parties a partial divorce. They must live apart, but the marriage is not dissolved until a divorce is granted.

Separation Agreement: The legal document listing provisions for peace between divorcing couples, division of property, spousal support, and responsibility for children of the marriage. The couple's agreement or court-ordered terms are part of the divorce decree.

Service: Providing a copy of the papers being filed to the opposing party.

Settlement Agreement: A written contract dividing property, spelling out rights and obligations, and settling issues such as spousal and child support and custody.

Six Month Rule: Provision of the Child Contingency Rule that states when the spousal support payments are to be reduced not more than six months before or after the date on which the child reaches 18, 21, or the age of majority in their state. (IRS Code Section 71(c)(2))

Sole Custody: The custodial parent has the power to make all decisions, both day-to-day and major decisions concerning the child's health, education, and welfare without consulting or notifying the non-custodial parent.

Spousal Support: Money paid by one spouse to the other for the recipient's support following the divorce. Support may be mandated for a specific period of time (long-term or short-term) and is based on the needs of the recipient, ability to pay, and economic differences between the partners. Also called alimony or maintenance. See "Section 71" (above) for IRS guidelines.

Spousal Support Recapture: Under Internal Revenue Code (IRC) §71, recapture requirements apply if excess alimony (also commonly known as "spousal support") payments are front-loaded into the first three post-separation years.

Spouse: Husband or wife.

Standard of Living: A factor when determining spousal support, allowing the recipient an adequate amount to maintain their current lifestyle.

Stipulation: An agreement between the parties or their counsel, usually related to matters of procedure.

Subpoena: A court order requiring a person's appearance in court or at a deposition as a witness or to present documents or other evidence for a case.

Summons: A Summons is a written notification to the defendant or respondent that an action has been filed against him or her. It notifies a spouse of his/her rights and obligations in responding to the Complaint for Divorce.

Tax Debt: For three years after a divorce, the IRS can perform random audits of joint tax returns. The divorce agreement should provide instructions and where the money should come from if an audit is involved.

Tax Reform Act of 1976: This Act permitted spousal support to be deductible in arriving at adjusted gross income so that the tax payer who does not itemize deductions may nevertheless deduct spousal support.

Tax Reform Act of 1984 (TRA): TRA added Code Sec. 1041, which allows marital property to be transferred back and forth between spouses without creating any tax on the transfer. The income tax basis of each asset is the basis of the asset in the hands of the transferor. TRA simplified the definition of spousal support, and it prevents property settlements from being disguised as spousal support.

Temporary Orders: Orders granting relief between the filing of the lawsuit and the judgment. Temporary orders are automatic in some states. They are also called Pendente Lite Orders.

Testimony: Statements under oath by a witness in a court hearing or deposition.

Transcripts: The written record of the divorce proceedings, testimony, or depositions.

Trial: The time when a judge hears the contested permanent or temporary issues, with supporting evidence and witnesses, in a couple's divorce decisions. The judge may take a few hours or a few weeks to review the information presented and issue a court opinion.

Uncontested Divorce: When the defendant is not going to try to stop the divorce and there are no issues for the court to decide about the children, money, or property.

Unsecured Debt: A loan that is not secured by an underlying asset. Unsecured debt includes credit cards, personal bank loans, lines of credit, and loans from family or friends.

Venue: The county in which the case is heard.

Vesting: In a retirement account, "vesting" means ownership. If an employee is "fully vested," he/she owns 100% of the account balance. When an employee is "partially vested," he/she is only entitled to a specified percentage of the employer's contributions. Employee contributions are always 100% vested. Depending on the plan type, employer contributions have different vesting requirements.

Visitation: The right of the non-custodial parent to see the children. Increasingly, states are granting this right to grandparents and close relatives.

Voir Dire: Where the opposing counsel has the opportunity to disqualify an expert witness.

Writ of Summons: A form issued by the court directing a party to respond to a complaint, motion, or petition.

NOTES

NOTES

CPSIA information can be obtained
at www.ICGtesting.com
Printed in the USA
BVOW10s0713050516

446676BV00005B/8/P